Walks in Mysterious South Lakeland

Graham Dugdale

Published by Sigma Leisure – an imprint of
Sigma Press, 1 South Oak Lane, Wilmslow, Cheshire SK9 6AR, England.

British Library Cataloguing in Publication Data
A CIP record for this book is available from the British Library.

ISBN: 1-85058-589-X

Typesetting and Design by: Sigma Press, Wilmslow, Cheshire.

Cover photograph: the mist-shrouded summit of Black Combe, from Windmill Hill, a mile south-east of Broughton-in-Furness *(Graham Dugdale)*

Maps and photographs: Graham Dugdale

Printed by: MFP Design and Print

Disclaimer: the information in this book is given in good faith and is believed to be correct at the time of publication. No responsibility is accepted by either the author or publisher for errors or omissions, or for any loss or injury howsoever caused. Only you can judge your own fitness, competence and experience.

Preface

"The unknown is ever imagined"

Greek Proverb

With a historical tradition stretching back into the depths of a hazy past, it comes as no surprise that all manner of legends have grown up to enhance the allure of the Lake District. Intrigue and mystery have always stimulated feverish debate in this most fascinating of National Parks, none more so than when fact and fantasy merge into a nebulous homogeneity.

Some ghostly apparitions can be explained away logically. A trick of the light, or the sound of wind howling through the trees. When recounted over a tankard of ale, such experiences can soon assume exaggerated proportions. Passed down through generations often by word of mouth, outlandish folktales probably had a simple and logical origin.

But some of the freakish coincidences in which you are about to take part have no easy explanation. Why do men of sound mind and body refuse to sleep in the notorious *Tapestry Room* at Muncaster Castle? Did a single man actually lift a gigantic beam into place at Kentmere Hall? And did the spring at Humphrey Head really improve the health of miners?

Certainly much of our colourful past is based on events that have been honed and fine tuned as they adapt to changing circumstances. Smugglers were the main culprits for inventing bizarre occurrences to stave off the long arm of the revenue men. In times when superstition and mythology were not so easily shrugged off by a gullible populace, such tales flourished, becoming magnified in the telling. Lanty Slee of Little Langdale was just such a character.

Yet others are fully documented and have become an accepted part of local history. Criminal activities especially make for exciting explorations, adding that essential touch of spice to walks that are no less enjoyable in their own right. Gibbets and hanging trees, for example, send a chilling shiver down the spine when confronted at close quarters.

So what is the fine line which irrevocably marks the divergence of truth from fiction? Make up your own mind after sampling these mysterious walks and experiencing at first hand the quaint, the quirky and the downright bizarre phenomena that are as much a feature of local culture as Cumberland Sausage.

Unexplained phenomena and skulduggery of every description make exciting quests that can but stimulate the curiosity of travellers in Lakeland. Scoff at the notions put forward if you must. Enter haunted places with trepidation by all means. But most of all, savour and appreciate this countryside that is second to none. And if you gain half as much delectation in the process as I did, you will indeed be have travelled far on the road to self enlightenment.

Acknowledgements

Many thanks to Philip Cavener of NeeBee Boots for his continued support and supply of CBX boots.

Don Cooper of Lowe Alpine in Kendal is also to be commended for providing one of their top-of-the-range Airmesh rucksacks.

Jeff and Nancy Waine of Murthwaite Farm in Longsleddale were kind enough to show me round their home whilst investigating the infamous Dr Lickbarrow. A much appreciated mug of tea was no less welcome.

Peter Frost Pennington, General Manager of Muncaster Castle, was kind enough to inform me of the strange occurrences that have made this residence so receptive to paranormal activity

Graham Dugdale

Contents

The Walks

The walks in this book are graded according to the effort involved, in terms of distance covered and height ascended. This makes no concession to personal preference, which would most certainly be open to dispute in any case.

Only five of the walks visit mountain summits which exceed 2000 feet. A mere 30 feet short of the magic figure, the Dark Sentinel of Whicham merits inclusion in this group. Perhaps it should be emphasised at this point that on both fell and footpath, I refuse to think metric. No bewitching connotation can be attached to a height of 610 metres (2000 feet). This stubborn streak has been curtailed, however, in the written descriptions – so feet, yards and metres are all included. This is more to encourage younger walkers to whom *feet* are those strange-shaped appendages that fit into your boots.

The majority of mysterious happenings have taken place at lower altitudes. Ghosts are gregarious entities that rarely venture onto the lonely fell tops and the myths and legends surrounding bizarre events are primarily associated with the periphery where the storytellers dwelt. In consequence, they are eminently suitable for all the family to enjoy whilst learning more about the origins of our Lakeland heritage. Armchair explorers and those who simply relish the opportunity to delve beneath the surface are well catered for.

Paths and Maps

Once the public highways are left behind, rights-of-way are made use of at all times. They are marked in green on the relevant Ordnance Survey maps, the walks being designed to start and finish at the same point. Although many of these locations are to be found in remote outposts where a car is essential, a significant number can still be reached by public transport.

A sketch map is provided for each walk, though it is recommended to always take the relevant Ordnance Survey map on any walk in the Lake District. On the following two pages you will find a map to assist in the easy location of the walks and a key to identify the symbols used on the sketch maps.

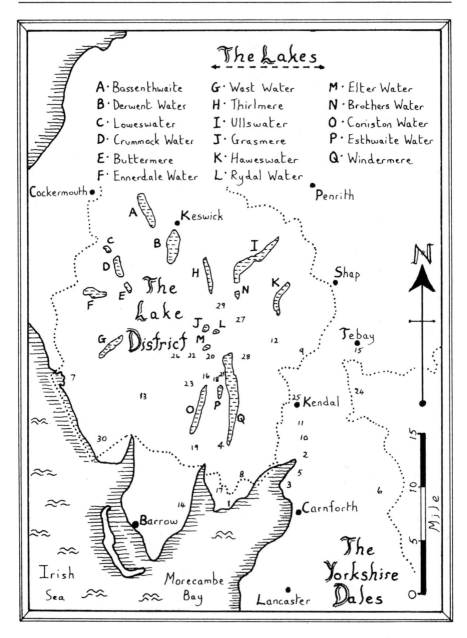

Location Map: numbers refer to walks in this book

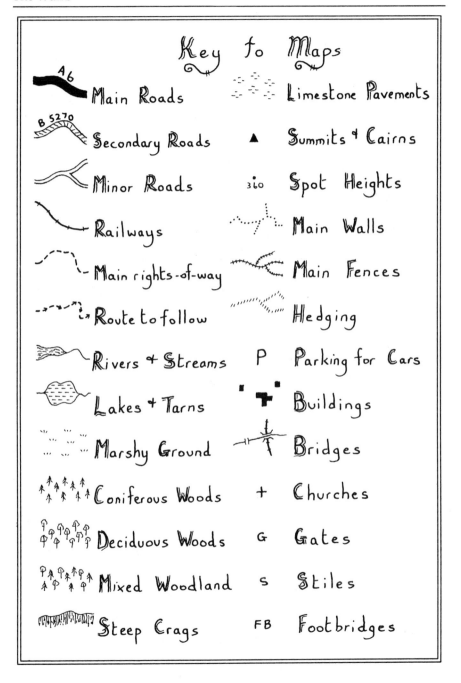

Key to Maps

A6 Main Roads

B 5270 Secondary Roads

Minor Roads

Railways

Main rights-of-way

Route to follow

Rivers + Streams

Lakes + Tarns

Marshy Ground

Coniferous Woods

Deciduous Woods

Mixed Woodland

Steep Crags

Limestone Pavements

▲ Summits + Cairns

360 Spot Heights

Main Walls

Main Fences

Hedging

P Parking for Cars

Buildings

Bridges

+ Churches

G Gates

S Stiles

FB Footbridges

1. Of Wolf and Water

Mysteries:	Holy Well Spa, GR 390739. Wraysholme Wolf, GR 383754. *Belladonna Atropa*, GR 389745
Distance:	4½ miles
Total height climbed:	150 feet/46 metres
Nearest centre:	Allithwaite
Start & finish:	The tiny village of Allithwaite lies on the B5277 between Grange-over-Sands and Flookburgh. Pull off the main road down a narrow cul-de-sac on the left 50 metres beyond the Pheasant Inn. Park on the right verge.
Maps:	Ordnance Survey 1:25000 Pathfinder 636 sheet, Grange-over-Sands.

Thrusting deep into the mud flats of Morecambe Bay like a Zulu assegai, the promontory of Humphrey Head is unique in being the only coastal headland composed of limestone in the north-west. Its reputation as the last bastion of wolves in Cumbria has now been usurped in favour of a more botanical distinction.

The woodland covering the flanks of the Head is home to a myriad of wild flowers. Rare plants such as Rock Samphire, Spiked Speedwell, Pellitory of the Wall, Dropwort and Maidenhair Fern are all represented. None is more sinister than the Deadly Nightshade. Also known as Belladonna, its dark-veined flesh tinted leaves thrive in the darkened recesses of the woods exuding a deathly poison. Rabbits have frequently been seen chomping with impunity on the virulent leaves. However, on no account should you follow their example.

Extracted for atropine, as used in opthalmics, this substance was used in Renaissance Italy as an eye cosmetic. Enlarged pupils certainly had the desired effect on suitors by making these dusky ladies more alluring, but with the detriment of being unable to focus properly. Who could imagine that with such a lethal pedigree, *Belladonna Atropa* is a close relation of the unassuming potato.

The Walk

From the back lane in Allithwaite, return to the main road, taking the side lane which forks right of the Pheasant Inn. At the bottom of Jack Hill, bear right through the yard of Blenket Farm using two gates at either end. Follow a clear track with a hedge on the right. This soon arcs to the left accompanying another somewhat 'gappy' hedge. Watch for an obscured stile in the hedge on the right at the end of this field. At this point, our route leaves this clear track to follow a hedged dyke.

Indeed, the vast majority of field boundaries in this area are hedges rather than fences or walls. On the left, the limestone knoll of Kirkhead with its distinctive old tower dominates the foreground. After passing the next stile, take note of the iron railings on the left which contain the redundant sewage works. This has now been replaced by the current facility operated by North-west Water and located nearer the sea.

Cross a footbridge with attendant stile but take heed of the battery-operated electric fence adjoining the dyke. Designed to incarcerate wandering animals, it can be likened to the eighth sign of the zodiac in having a nasty sting in its tail. Another hedge stile follows, after which the right-of-way crosses the sewage works access road located behind a protective fence on the left.

Continue alongside the dyke to pass under the railway and so on to Wyke Farm. A wall stile is immediately followed by a set of stone steps which deposit you on the sea shore. Marshy reed beds stretch away into the distance between Kirkhead End and Humphrey Head. Stay close to the sea wall along a sandy path above the high water mark.

After 200 metres, the footpath over to the west side of Humphrey Head is passed. If the tide has been in recently, the salt marsh is likely to be waterlogged. Pick a route along the limestone slabs to reach the southern edge of the woods. A rusty oil drum (Summer 1996), or red/white/blue nature reserve marking on a stone pillar, indicates the start of the woodland trail.

Paralleling the coastline, this narrow tortuous trod is a joy to walk as it snakes amongst the natural sconces of trees and shrubbery. For those who relish the containing influence of the sylvan screen, the next half mile should be savoured at a languid pace. Too soon, the fence stile at the northern limit is crossed and the perimeter fence around the Head followed to its extremity. Cross to the far side and explore the exposed rocky promontory that forms the spear point of Humphrey Head.

In all directions barring due north, the flat expanse of sand stretches

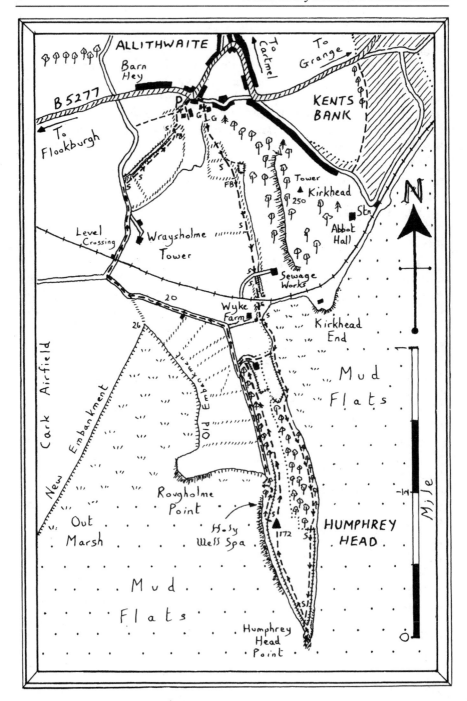

away across Morecambe Bay. From Kents Bank to Hest Bank on the Lancashire side, regular trips follow the old coaching route – but only at low tide. In view of the shifting nature inherent in the sands and channels, the eight-mile crossing must only be undertaken under the supervision of an official guide.

Most celebrated is Cedric Robinson, who received an honorary MSc from Lancaster University in July of 1996 for 33 years of unceasing effort as the Queen's Guide to Morecambe Bay. Besides guiding thousands of people across the Bay, Cedric has to prepare detailed reports on the state of the sands for the Duchy of Lancaster trustees. Born and bred in Flookburgh, most of his life has been spent trawling the cockle beds in winter and netting the famous Morecambe Bay shrimps in summer. The annual fee of £15 received for being the official guide indicates that this service is performed as a labour of love.

Re-trace your steps to cross the stile and mount the easy gradient alongside the fence onto the summit of Humphrey Head. Being less than 200 feet (60 metres) in height, the ascent of this noble outlier is within the capabilities of anybody who has yet to receive their certificate from the Queen. A wall to the east contains the main spread of woodland. Gently shelving, it contrasts markedly with the western orbit, concealing the precipitate limestone cliff face.

A stile leads to a path following the rim, which should be followed if a swift descent to the base of the Head is sought. At the end of the otherwise impassable rock wall, a distinct route picks a twisted course down through the tree cover. Steep it certainly is, although perfectly feasible if due care is exercised. At the upper edge, constant usage has smoothed the limestone outcrops and loosened the stony trail. Take it slow and easy and no problems should be encountered.

For those who doubt their ability to descend by this route, the less exciting option is to maintain a northerly course along the crest. An easy gradient slants down past the outdoor pursuits centre to meet the Cross Fell track. Keep left to reach the shore road.

Even at the height of summer, this special locale is rarely crowded. Yet in the 19th century, many people came to imbibe the waters of the Holy Well Spa that issued from the cliff face. Cartmel doctors encouraged their patients to drink deep claiming that a "quick purging would bring return to health".

The mineral water, said to contain over twenty different salts, was dispensed from a fisherman's cottage which has now completely disappeared. Only a plastic pipe with a caveat advising visitors not to drink now remains of the spa whose curative properties were once renowned far and wide.

Most assuredly, the local scene in the 1840s would have been substantially diverse. Queues of participants eager to sample this prime elixir were more than willing to pay a cost of two old pence per cup. Lead miners from Alston in County Durham visited Humphrey Head to drink the restorative for over forty years. Modern analysis has assigned a mildly laxative effect to the spring water, which perhaps helped to flush the lead out of their system.

Embankments are being improved along the coastline to the west of the Head as protection for the rich farmland against flooding. At Rougholme Point, the original shoreline offers a rare opportunity for geology enthusiasts to examine the exposed strata of Bockram. Composed of an amalgam of sandstone, limestone and ringed fossils known as *St Cuthbert's Beads*, this unusual rock formation dates back over 130 million years to the Permian Age.

After a suitable exploration along the shoreline, do not be tempted to clamber up the exposed rock face unless you aspire to the fate of ten-year-old William Pedder. This unfortunate lad met a sad and terminal end at the foot of the cliffs on 22 August 1857 at the spot marked by a carved remembrance stone.

Leave the shore area to make a leisurely stroll north along the access road. At the same time, keep an eye open among the shady rank of trees on the right for sign of the Deadly Nightshade which thrives hereabouts. Remember that consuming *five* of the plant's berries will rapidly consign you to the happy hunting grounds of your esteemed ancestors.

The first road on the right leads up to the outdoor centre and is followed after a further 200 metres by the lane serving Wyke Farm and the new sewage works. Slant left here across the coastal plain for half a mile, turning right at the next T-junction. Beyond the open level crossing on the right stands the grey edifice of Wraysholme Tower.

An impressive pele tower and a defensive site, it was home to the locally honoured Harrington family in the middle ages. Legend suggests that John, the handsome son of Sir Edgar Harrington, fell madly in love with his father's beautiful ward, Adela. Upon discovering this, Sir Edgar was consumed with a fearsome rage and immediately disinherited his son and banished him from the estate. In despair, John left to join the Crusades against the Infidel.

Returning secretly some years later, he found that a rampant wolf had been terrorising the district. Sir Edgar had offered the hand of his ward in marriage to any knight who could dispatch the savage beast. Eventually cornering the exhausted wolf on the shore below Humphrey Head, John slew it and claimed the hand of his loved one together with his lost inheritance.

Although this was the last wolf to be seen in Lakeland, it was not until the reign of Elizabeth I some three hundred years later that these wild creatures were finally eradicated.

After passing the entrance to Wraysholme Farm, watch for a stile on the right pointing the way back to Allithwaite across the fields. Beyond the second stile, accompany a fence on your left alongside a reedy dyke until a footbridge enables you to cross to the far side. Bear right along a wide track aiming left of a pair of cottages to reach the car.

An easy walk, yet one that is full of intrigue and interest. The legend and the natural attraction of Humphrey Head blend well in a simple harmony that is a delight to meet.

2. Myths Around Milnthorpe

Mysteries: Belvedere Cottage, GR 500815. The Cappel, GR 500802. Kill-moulis, GR 496799

Distance: 7 miles

Total height climbed: insignificant

Nearest centre: Milnthorpe

Start & finish: Park in the village square at Milnthorpe, in front of the church.

Maps: Ordnance Survey 1:25000 Pathfinder 627, Milnthorpe, and 637 Burton-in-Kendal and Caton.

St Thomas's Church was named after its benefactor, Thomasina Rawlinson, when erected in 1837. Behind, on a rising slope, stands Belvedere Cottage, alone in its own grounds. A rather austere building of late Georgian origin, it is thought to have been built in the 1820s. It became the local vicarage in 1844 when the Reverend Nicholas Padwick lived there with his family until his retirement sixteen years later.

The good reverend's influence must have been considerable in view of his subsequent re-appearance during the tenancy of his successor, Frederick Raikes. It has been suggested that a poverty-stricken retirement was the cause of this resurrection, although nothing definite is known. What certainly has been recognised are the numerous occasions on which the spectral materialisation of Padwick was witnessed by servants and gardeners, who must have found the experience unnerving to say the least.

In the 1920s, it was the turn of the Reverend Gamble's daughter to claim a sighting. Young Jennifer wanted to know why her father had entered the room wearing his full ecclesiastical regalia. This was the first time that her parents were made aware of the Victorian spirit that continued to haunt Belvedere (as it became known) until 1979.

When John Kelly assumed the role of vicar in that year and moved into the house, he took no chances by asking the Bishop of Penrith to conduct a private communion service inside the vicarage. It is significant that the ghost of *Old Nick* has not reappeared since.

The Walk

From the square, walk up the road on the right of the church. Join the course of the old road from Beetham, now barely discernible as such, through a stile to head south along a narrow fenced corridor behind some new houses. Entering the next field, the path follows a hedge past the primary school and behind another row of houses. At the far end of the village boundary, bear left, aiming for the far corner of the field.

Cross the corner of the next field through two stiles and thence alongside a hedge. The straight course of the path lies between two elongated hills with the shape of an upturned rowing boat. This area displays all the traits associated with the regular deposition of material by a glacier during the last Ice Age, around 8000 BC.

Orientated from north-east to south-west indicating the direction of ice movement, these domed hillocks known as *drumlins* are about a third of a mile in length and one hundred feet (30 metres) high. Between Old Hutton and Beetham, over forty can be identified. Referred to as "*basket of eggs*" topography, it may be less spectacular than the ice-sculpting that gives the heart of Lakeland its universal appeal, but is nonetheless a unique landscape possessing its own intrinsic character.

Continue south past a well that has been turned into a drinking trough for animals and onward to the field corner where a back lane is joined. This point marks the junction of what used to be the main road. Although difficult to envisage, our route so far was the main highway into Milnthorpe from the south. It diverged here, the right fork continuing north through the hamlet of Ackenthwaite.

On your left rises another drumlin unusual in sporting its own appendage, a testament to the significance attached to this particular hillock locally. Cappleside Hill is the sole reminder of a ferocious black hound that was said to terrorise late night travellers, many of whom spoke of blazing eyes red with the fires of hell. Known as the **Cappel**, the creature was thought to have lived in a barn at nearby Cappleside Hall (now demolished) where it assisted the farmer. Both locals and strangers claim to have been run off the property by this devil dog. Others said it often spoke with its master. Perhaps this was the reason for the Vicar of Beetham being summoned to exorcise the ogre before committing it to the waters of the River Bela for all eternity.

Once the Hall had fallen into disrepair at the end of the 17th century the mistress of the house, known as the *Cappleside Lady,* was reputed to haunt the ruins, although the reason for her spectral visitations remains a mystery.

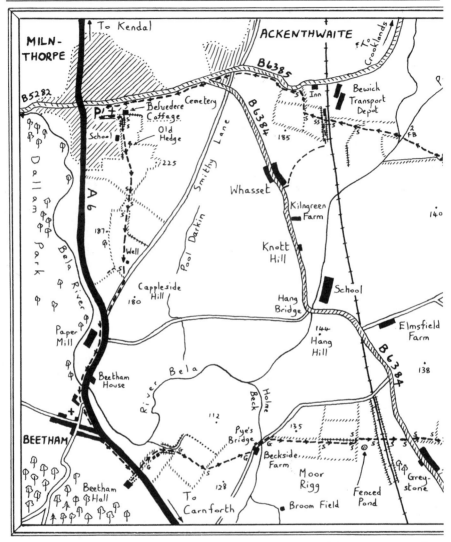

Join the A6, crossing over to make use of the paved foot-way past the modern paper mill and over the River Bela on the old road bridge. Turn aside to visit the site of Heron Corn Mill, which lies a quarter of a mile up the narrow lane on the side of the river.

Here, in a cave close to the weir, is said to live a particularly active boggle (a malignant spirit) by the name of Killmoulis. Supposedly without a mouth but sporting a mighty nose, this decidedly odd char-

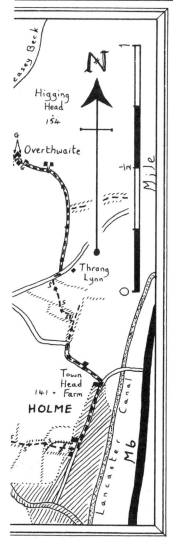

acter scatters ash among the grain when a malicious bent strikes him. Reputed to howl in sympathy when things go wrong at the mill, one wonders where such a sound could originate in view of the absence of the appropriate orifice.

Returning to the bridge over the Bela, the original course of the road through Beetham is clearly visible. Beyond the war memorial, stick with the main road as far as the access track serving Beetham Hall.

Go down the farm track immediately opposite past a pair of corrugated iron buildings angling right along the bank of a fenced dyke. Enter a field keeping straight ahead to make the next field over a fence stile mid way along a hedge. Reach the narrow lane at Beckside Farm by slanting half left.

Cross Holme Beck at Pye's Bridge leaving the lane at the next gate on the right. Mount the grass slope of the most southerly drumlin with a hedge on your right continuing due east to reach the railway. A stone ladder stile leads to the open track, arguably the most important thoroughbred line in Railtrack's depleted stable. Trains speed along this stretch, so take extra care when crossing.

Emerge onto the road just north of Greystone and cross straight over through a miniature sprung gate with a hedge on your right. After a series of three stiles, approach a new fence which appears to be for funnelling sheep towards Holme Farm. A further set of three brings you to the edge of Holme. Entering the yard of by means of an ingeniously spring-loaded gate, the next thirty metres must be negotiated with care but at a brisk pace.

Beware the black beast that here lies in wait for the unwary rambler.

A noisy fearsome brute, it is not averse to testing its canines on any tasty leg within reach. Could this be the *Cappel* which has taken up residence in Holme now that its old abode is no more?

Having safely reached the far side, turn north along the linear street for a quarter of a mile, as far as the left fork at Town Head Farm. This marks the northern extremity of Holme village. Follow the narrow lane for another quarter mile continuing straight ahead along a rough hedged track when the lane bends sharp left. Watch for a stile on the left after 200 metres which allows ingress to the adjacent field.

It is worth noting that virtually all the field boundaries on this walk are composed of well-kept hedges. Since the decline of indigenous woodland to make way for agricultural usage, hedging has become the principal habitat in which wildlife can flourish. Stone walls and fences cannot claim to be anywhere near as environmentally friendly when it comes to providing a suitable ambience in which our furred and feathered friends can dwell.

The path circumvents the field where another stile is located. Cross the next field to its corner, arriving at a back lane. Turn right and almost immediately left along the metalled access road serving Overthwaite where the right-of-way circles right around the farm buildings. After passing through a pair of wide steel gates, cross over a stepped wall stile and stick with a narrow trail between a large slurry tank and barn.

Cross the next field heading west towards the River Bela at its junction with Peasey Beck. Two footbridges enable these substantial waterways to be negotiated with dry feet. Thereafter, maintain a westerly course over one ladder stile to reach the railway. Again, it is necessary to **Stop, Look and Listen!** Encouraging train drivers to practice their 'emergency stop' routine is not to be recommended.

On your right, untidy workshops and the Transport Depot are a blot on an otherwise idyllic rustic scene. Ignore them by pressing on across a fenced track into the opposite field. Cross to the far side where a step stile is climbed before heading north around the right-hand edge of a drumlin to reach the B6385.

Turn left through the tiny village of Ackenthwaite and so back into Milnthorpe. You are unlikely to be disturbed on this walk by others of the human species, except when passing through the settlements en route. Enjoy the tranquillity of this green and pleasant land, including the remarkable herd of drumlins thereon, at the same time reflecting on the strange fate of Nicholas Padwick.

3. Around Gaits Barrow

Mystery:	Hawes Water, GR 478766
Distance:	5 miles
Total height climbed:	Insignificant
Nearest centre:	Silverdale
Start & finish:	An official car park on the north side of the road between Red Bridge and Silverdale.
Maps:	Ordnance Survey 1:25000 Pathfinder Series 636, Grange-over-Sands.

Encompassing two important wetland nature reserves, this walk lies within the Silverdale/Arnside AONB (Area of Outstanding Natural Beauty). Smaller than a National Park, this is one of a number of designated orbits which were established to protect vulnerable stretches of countryside that lie outside the strict auspices of their larger cousins. No one who has visited this select corner of England can deny its place within a rural utopia.

Limestone pavements, fluted and tinted with a myriad shades of grey, blend with the sylvan screen. Unlike the Lake District with its rugged display of grandeur, there is little within this subdued Lilliputian terrain that can be recalled in graphic detail.

Its inherent attraction stems from a lack of regularity. Woody allotments and open pasture orchestrate in syncopated harmony with craggy outcrops and mossland. Such easy-going landscape is a pleasure to experience.

The Walk

From the car park secreted amid a narrow copse, make your way back along the road towards Red Bridge. Take the footpath on the left which starts 100 metres beyond the road junction. Following a wall initially, the main railway line serving Barrow and West Cumbria is soon crossed – and with great care naturally. Thereafter, the faint path parallels the fence alongside the reed-choked sweep of Hawes Water Moss.
Pass through a gap in the hedge to climb a grassy bank leading up to

Hayeswater – home of a mythical dragon

Challon Hall. Once over the wall stile, the right-of-way enters the Hall grounds alongside the outbuildings now refurbished and converted into holiday apartments. Turn right along the back lane towards Arnside forking right along a clear track after 100 metres.

Beyond the gate, the path follows a charming course through the deciduous canopy adjoining Hawes Water. Watch for a track on the right which leads down to the water's edge past a strange one-roomed abode. Now devoid of a roof and boarded up, one can only speculate as to its original purpose.

Approaching the fringe of this enchanted pool, keep a wary open for strange creatures skulking amidst the reed scarf that surrounds the silver sheen. Largest of the four tarns in the area, Hawes Water is renowned for its char, a fish of the trout family. One can only wonder whether this Lakeland delicacy has helped to sustain a more sinister resident of the mere.

In days of yore, when the *Dragon of Hawes Water* turned the peaceful mere into a potent ferment, local people could expect trouble and discord to invade their humble community. This vile beast was likened to a worm and was said to have been cast into the tarn by a certain Roger

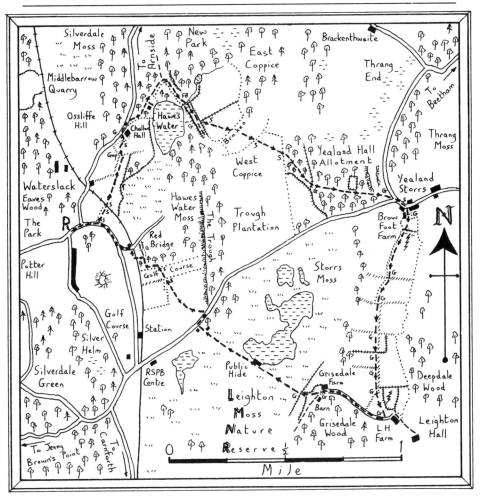

de Conyers as a reminder of his dragon-slaying prowess. In the County of Durham, this brave knight had exterminated many dragons which terrorised the villages and preyed upon children and young maidens who strayed to close to their dens.

Roger eventually married the daughter of landowner William de Lancaster and is thought to have cast at least one baby worm into the tarn which grew to full size. How many of these fearsome brutes occupy the dark pool today, however, is not known.

If dragon spotting is not on your agenda for the day, return to the main path and continue north. Circle around the top end of the tarn to head down the opposite side noting the limestone scar on your left. The path opens into a fenced corridor after crossing a rough stone bridge.

On the right, a small gate allows access to the edge of the tarn which is clear of reeds on this eastern shore. The lime rich soil is ideal for Marl grassland and its dry consistency encourages the Bird's Eye Primrose to flourish. In summer, the delicate pink blooms add a welcome splash of colour to the verdant setting.

A little further along the main path, watch for a stile on the left. This allows passage across the open field, over a broken wall, and thence to a substantial wall climbed by a ladder stile. Continue in a direct line across the middle of the next field, towards a stile at its far side. Nobody can fail to be inspired by the stunning view southward across the broad tract of Leighton Moss bird sanctuary supported by the pastel backdrop across Morecambe Bay.

Turn right to follow a clear track through an irregular sprinkling of hawthorn trees until a fence is reached. Beyond the gate, a direct course heading due east through the enclosed thicket of Yealand Hall Allotment will bring you to the road junction close to Yealand Storrs. Taking a short walk of about 200 metres through the settlement, look out for a narrow wall gap signposted to Leighton Hall.

Pass to the left of Brow Foot Farm through the first gate, after which the grass concourse takes a wide sweep to the right. Where it homes in towards the right side of the field, beware of an electrified cow barrier blocking the right-of-way (when I reconnoitred this route). Although only a single strand of wire which is easily negotiated, protection of one's nether regions must be considered a priority if a *shocking* experience is to be avoided.

Keep a count of the gates along this stretch of the walk – open or closed – which should number eight in total en route to Home Farm. At the end, bear right down the metalled lane serving Grisedale Farm before it changes to a rough track immediately beyond the farm gate.

Fork right to follow a fence around to the edge of Leighton Moss which is crossed by an arrow straight causeway constructed above the level of the surrounding wetlands. Tall banks of reed and willow severely restrict the view across the reserve until the public viewing hide is reached. Take time out to sit awhile inside and observe the fascinating manoeuvres practised by our feathered colleagues across the open mere.

Since its inception in 1889, the RSPB (Royal Society for the Protection of Birds) has set up over one hundred reserves with Leighton Moss being instituted in 1964. Intensive management of the 400 acre site ensures protection for all birds and other wildlife that choose to set down here. Rare species such as the bittern are able to breed and thrive in the ideal medium of reed fen interspersed with scrub willow.

Continual scything of the reed beds is essential to prevent their encroachment into the open meres which vary between six inches (15cm) and three feet (about a metre) in depth. Once an inlet of the sea, an embankment at the mouth of Leighton Moss has enabled regeneration to take place in a controlled environment.

Although red and roe deer are often seen within the vicinity of the local woods, you will be lucky indeed to catch sight of another sporadic visitor, namely the otter. Gliding through the still water in search of eels, these graceful mammals will normally be sighted at dusk along with another infrequent visitor who sports a black and white face mask. Look for their footprints in the mud banks adjacent to entry points for the meres along the central causeway.

Those who wish to learn more about the work of the RSPB should turn left for a quarter of a mile, down the road at the far side of the Moss to visit the centre which now occupies Myers Farm. Return to the access track and take the path on the left which can be located 100 metres beyond. Bear half left on a north-westerly point slanting down to a stile at the field corner. Here it is necessary to cross the fairway of Silverdale Golf Course. Although a right-of-way, keep a beady eye open for flying balls.

Aim for the wall stile to the left of a steel barred gate. After joining a major track, turn left along this but watch for a narrow indistinct left turn as you approach a padlocked gate at the end of the track. A ladder access enables the railway to be crossed 100 metres south of Red Bridge. Mount the steps opposite which will bring you to the back lane crossing the bridge.

Head left up to the main road and there turn right for a return to the car park. If a broad spectrum of wildlife interests you, this will have been the perfect walk. Embracing the nature reserves of Gaits Barrow and Leighton Moss, you will be amply recompensed for the minimum effort involved. Dragon spotters, however, may be in for a protracted wait if their exigencies are to be catered for.

4. Finsthwaite Secret

Mystery: Home to a Princess, GR 368878

Distance: 3 miles

Total height climbed: 400 feet/122 metres

Nearest centre: Newby Bridge

Start & finish: In Newby Bridge, parking is limited to the side lane forking left off the Lakeside road after crossing the bridge over the River Leven. Various small pull-ins are available. No such restrictions exist if you intend making use of the railway.

Maps: Ordnance Survey Pathfinder 626, 1:25000, Broughton-in-Furness and Newby Bridge sheet.

Located one mile south of Lake Windermere, Newby Bridge grew up where the River Leven could most easily be crossed. During the Ice Age, the original lake glacier stopped for a period at Newby Bridge depositing end moraine and the creation of a lake. Infilling has since led to the formation of flat valley pastures as the lake has retreated back to Lakeside.

Before the building of the first bridge, the Leven was crossed at nearby Tinker's Ford. Passage across the river was quite safe, being only one metre deep at this point. That was so long as travellers avoided the perfidious *Dog Hole* in the middle. Some even thought the hidden fissure was bottomless.

The tinker in question was drowned here whilst making the crossing with a heavy load strapped to his back. Upon discovery, the unfortunate man was found to be standing in the upright position, but completely submerged. Not exactly a bottomless hole, but dangerous in the extreme for those careless enough to disregard the warnings.

Today Newby Bridge is dominated by the large Swan Hotel complex which has taken advantage of this important bridging point. When approaching from the east, it is the dense blanket of woodland mantling these lower southern slopes that captures the eye. Composed of Silurian Slates which are less resistant to erosion than the volcanic rocks forming the core, this subdued terrain lacks the dramatic impact associated with the heartland. As such, the walking is easier and less cluttered by others of the species.

A novel and extremely gratifying way to complete this particular walk is to make use of the Lakeside-Haverthwaite Steam Railway. Parking at Haverthwaite, catch the train to Newby Bridge Halt for the start of the walk, returning along the full 3½ miles from Lakeside.

Maintained by a small permanent staff supported by volunteer helpers, this is the only privately owned standard gauge railway in Cumbria. A branch line from the main Furness Railway, it was closed to passengers in 1965. Total closure followed two years later after the demise of the ironworks at Backbarrow. Originally, it was hoped to establish a scenic route all the way from Ulverston, but the new road improvement scheme effectively scuppered that notion. Not until 1973 was the current 112-year-old line from Haverthwaite re-opened to the public.

The Walk

After alighting at the pleasantly refurbished halt at Newby Bridge, retrace your steps to the bridge over the railway. Below on the opposite hand lies Water Side House, which is where the heroine of this walk resided during her brief sojourn in the area. More of this fascinating story will be revealed when we reach St Peter's Church at Finsthwaite.

Now walk back down the lane to Newby Bridge and take the first left across the railway. Turn immediately left at the far side up a rough lane serving a number of private residences. On your right is a new public footpath signposted to Finsthwaite Tower. Only those with energy in abundance or kryptonite in their veins should consider attempting this ascent to the old abandoned summer house, a return by the same route being necessary.

Open to the sky, the crenellated square monument was erected in 1799 to the memory of those serving in the Royal Navy. A stone tablet high on the wall commemorates the seafarers "*whose matchless conduct and irresistible valour decisively defeated the fleets of France, Spain and Holland and preserved and protected liberty and commerce*".

At that period in our history, the tower must have been in plain view, a symbol of England's prestige and maritime invincibility. Such displays of pride have largely disappeared, along with the tower which is concealed within extensive growth and easily missed.

Having returned to the bottom, superhumans who regularly eat three shredded wheat for breakfast can now continue up the lane to a stile before entering the wooded enclave of Wintering Park. During the hunting season, keep an ear open for the deep bark of shotguns as this is pheasant country. Erring from the designated right-of-way is, therefore, not to be recommended.

Mount the increasingly steep slope on a clear path. The gradient eases just before a gap in the wall is passed through. Soon after, enter an open field by a wall stile. Stick to the left edge along a corridor bounded by an electric fence on the right. Disguised as a well-worn string vest, it packs a jarring punch for those who stray too close.

At the far end, more corpulent ramblers are assisted through the narrow slab stile by a newly positioned foot piece. Make for the far right corner of this field where a ladder stile assists onward progress. Maintain a course slightly west of north across a stepped wall stile before slanting down to Finsthwaite. A gate allows access to the paved forecourt of St Peter's Church.

Designated as an *inspired* church on the Ordnance Survey map, rather does it resemble a tower boasting a conical hat. Unusual and intriguing, nonetheless. A somewhat over-ambitious graveyard surrounds the noble edifice and our specific objective can be found inconspicuously secreted at the rear.

Here, Clementina Johannes Sobieski Douglass occupies a modest plot that may easily pass unnoticed. It

The grave of Princess Clementina

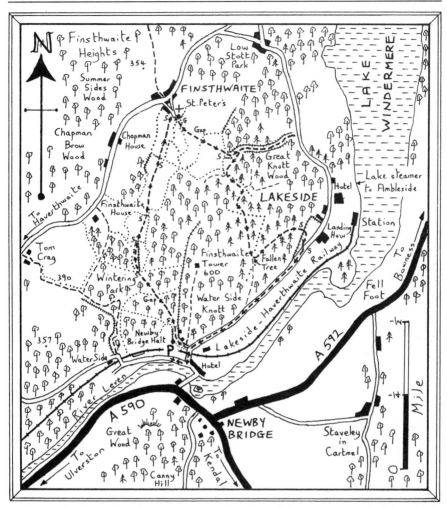

is devoid of garish adornment save for the white cross erected in 1913. So who, you may well ask, is the mysterious lady who was buried here in 1771?

Reputed to be the daughter of Charles Edward Stuart, better known as "Bonny Prince Charlie", baby Clementina arrived at Water Side in 1745 in the charge of two servants. It is said that her mother had nursed the wounded Charles after the Battle of Falkirk when he still entertained hopes of securing the English crown for his father.

History students will recall that his tartan army of 6000 clansmen marched south as far as Derby during the Scottish rebellion of 1745. Forced to retreat in the face of overwhelming odds, the "Young Pretender's" dream of royal conquest was finally crushed forever at the Battle of Culloden. Fleeing to Skye disguised as the maid of Flora MacDonald, Charles Stuart eventually reached safety in France. Perhaps the hurried retreat following the uprising and his subsequent pursuit as a fugitive made it impossible for Charles to collect his daughter.

Known locally as "a princess with wonderful fair hair", her name derives from the Polish royal ancestry on her grandmother's side with Douglass being the name Charles assumed when travelling incognito. The engraving at the foot of the tombstone, *Behold thy king cometh*, is a prophetic reminder that had the "45 rebellion" succeeded, Clementina could well have become Queen of England.

Another salutary reflection as you return to the lane concerns the plight of young mill apprentices who walked the 6 mile round trip twice every Sunday from Backbarrow Mill to worship in the church. During the early years of the 19th century, the harsh conditions in which children were forced to live and work until the age of 21 eventually resulted in legislation governing conditions of employment in factories. Perhaps some of the gravestones conceal grim stories of an industrial heritage achieved at considerable social cost.

After passing beneath the splendid lych gate, turn left past the old school house. Go through a gate to cross a field heading south-east towards Great Knott Wood. The path continues straight through an un-gated gap in the next wall, aiming for a hidden track entering the forest. A stile and an oddly-sited bench mark the start of a clear fenced route heading east down to the Hawkshead road.

After the initial 50 metres, make a sharp hairpin to the right and accompany this forest trail, slanting left into the dense inner sanctum, mainly comprised of conifers. Ignore the first track on the right which skirts the edge of the wood. At a T-junction, bear right and stick with this path for a quarter of a mile.

Starved of light, the twilight world beneath the verdant canopy imbues a silence all of its own. Brown pine needles carpeting the ground beneath embolden the sepulchral ambience. Where the life-giving sun penetrates the foliage, settlements of bracken and grass quickly take advantage of this rare opportunity to colonise the forest.

Watch out for the abrupt left-hander waymarked but now obscured by a fallen tree. The thin track that continues ahead should not be taken. Descend the steepening track to arrive at a fence stile. Beyond this, turn right along the edge of the wood to join the road back to Newby Bridge.

Should you wish to make use of the railway, turn left for Lakeside, there to catch the next train back to Haverthwaite. On passing Water Side House, spare a thought for the young princess who spent most of her brief life-span in residence. No doubt she frequently pondered on the truth behind her abandonment in this once remote corner of Cumbria, and the father who never returned.

5. In Step with the Fairies

Mysteries:	Hazelslack Tower, GR 477788. Fairy Steps, GR 487789
Distance:	4½ miles
Total height climbed:	275 feet/87 metres
Nearest centre:	Arnside
Start & finish:	A pull-in on the right immediately before the level crossing at Black Dyke.
Map:	Ordnance Survey 1:25000 Pathfinder Sheet 636 Grange-over-Sands.

The Walk

A light-hearted ramble, in keeping with the main objective, we begin at the pull-in immediately before the Black Dyke railway crossing by taking the path alongside an electricity sub-station. The stroll along the side of the railway line terminates after no more than a quarter of a mile when we bear right along the old Corpse Road.

Following a direct course over Whip Scar to Beetham, the track was originally engineered for the purpose of transporting the deceased from Arnside to the parish graveyard at Beetham Church.

In those days, the flat expanse of Arnside Moss was unfenced open grazing unlike today when the path is a narrow fenced causeway. The embankment carrying the B5282 and old dismantled railway prevents inundation by the tidal bore of the River Kent estuary. In centuries past, before the excavation of drainage dykes, the passage across the Moss must have been rather damp on foot. Today, the reclamation provides good quality pasture for sheep and cattle to graze upon.

A small footbridge across the first dyke is followed by a substantial wooden affair across Leighton Beck. It was constructed by Roy Whiting in 1995 with financial assistance from the *Friends of the Lake District*. Pass through a gate at the far side of the bridge. After which the path lies across open grassland which is drained by a series of dykes feeding into the main watercourse, and thence out to sea.

Ancient rights-of-way, especially those used for such a macabre purpose, provide us with a fascinating insight into the lives of residents.

After crossing the Carr Bank road, make your way up the facing terrace between exposed blocks of rain washed limestone. Pass through a wall stile on the right followed immediately by another to reach the far side of the wall. The path soon joins a rough access road serving the Hazelslack caravan park.

Take particular note of the looming presence ahead as you near the back lane. Hazelslack Tower, gaunt and forbidding in its rustic setting, stands aloof from the main buildings that make up the tiny hamlet. The square pele tower that once afforded refuge and protection to this farming community, now presents a lifeless and decaying facade to the world. This once proud edifice has become a mere curiosity of a turbulent past long consigned to the history books.

Lakeland has many of these grey stone fortresses, most of which were built in the 14th century to combat frequent incursions by hostile invaders from north of the border. Certainly those sited in the north of the region were subject to molestation by the fierce Celtic tribes, but there is no evidence of warring factions having ventured so far south.

So the question arises as to why the cluster of pele towers at Beetham, Dallam, Sizergh, Arnside and Hazelslack was erected in the first place.

Hazelslack Tower – an ancient pele

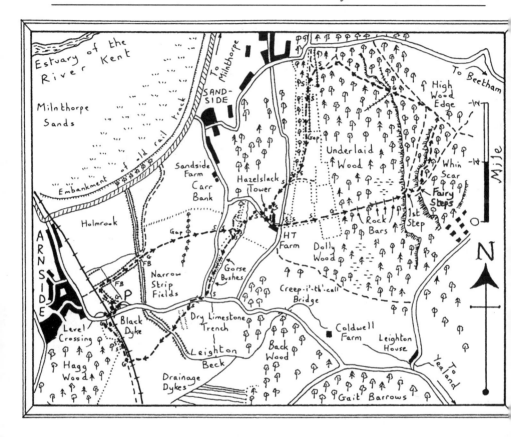

Perhaps it was the fear of what might be after listening to the blood curdling tales of passing visitors. Or maybe a spirited attempt to thwart attacks by roving brigands sailing up the Kent estuary. Nobody really knows. Today, the only invaders likely to be abroad are those wielding cameras rather than claymores.

Hazelslack is more likely to be remembered for the lavish display of colour sported by the resident peacocks. These majestic birds enjoy complete freedom of movement and strut their stuff exuding a haughty disdain for human interlopers.

Cross the road next to Hazelslack Tower Farm and head east alongside a wall following a straight course into the extensive verdant screen of Underlaid Wood. Limestone rock bars provide a series of rising terraces cocooned within the twilight world of densely packed mixed woodland. An open pavement of moss shrouded clint blocks and deeply chiselled grikes festooned with fern and flowers mark the approach to the first of the major scars. Split by a broadly stepped fissure, this is not, however, the main object of our excursion which lies 100 metres above and beyond.

As the grey precipice of Whin Scar emerges from the eerie silence, it is little wonder that all manner of correspondents have theorised about the origin of the Fairy Steps. Slanting left, the narrow shaft points the way to the open headland above.

Being delightfully impish folk with a bewitching sense of fun, the fairies of Whin Scar ensure that all wishes made at the foot of the cleft will be granted. That is on the surety that one can succeed in skipping up the stairway without touching the sides. Being of diminutive stature, such an undertaking would be of little consequence to these enchanting creatures.

Legend suggests that only those with second sight are permitted to witness this amazing spectacle. Mere mortals must be content with gazing open-mouthed in the face of such a Herculean task. No doubt others who have claimed a sighting will have been found propping up the bar at the Wheatsheaf Hotel in Beetham.

Once the main route between Arnside and Beetham, the provision of a rope-way assisted commercial travellers with the carriage of heavy goods. Iron rings driven into the rock face, enabled them to haul sacks of flour, not to mention coffined cadavers, up this otherwise impassable barrier.

Having attained the shelf above Whin Scar, the sylvan screen thins appreciably to reveal a magnificent prospect west towards Arnside Knott. An ideal setting to linger awhile before heading north along the top edge of the Scar.

After a short distance, the path crosses a small grooved pavement before descending to meet the main route across Beetham Fell. Turn left here to enter a clearing, in the centre of which is located a walkers' cross-roads. Fork left along a narrow trail into the birch woodland passing through a gated fence abutting the Scar edge.

Continue down through Longtail Wood taking the second of the main tracks on the left. This leads down to a fence stile at the edge of the woods. Cross the field to its far left corner and make your way down a brief walled lane to the next field. Our route slants away from the fence towards a stile in the far right corner. Accompany a wall on your right around to a stile after which the road to Hazelslack is crossed.

Beyond another stile immediately opposite, cross the field to Hazelslack Tower Farm. A wall stile facing the ancient block house abuts a short farm access road. It is clear from this angle that the pele tower has at some time in the past been linked to a pitched roof extension now completely demolished.

It is necessary at this point to retrace your steps as far as the double stile just beyond the caravan park. After negotiating the first stile, follow a clear path meandering through a clump of prickly gorse on the right of a small rill. Emerging at a T-junction, head right for 100 metres and take the path opposite a cottage.

The grass trail takes a north-east course towards the railway embankment crossing an unusual dry limestone fringed trench en route. After merging with a substantial farm track, it heads on towards the railway a quarter of a mile distant. Passing underneath, turn immediately right and follow the path back towards Black Dyke.

At the first stile, the way forward is squeezed between Hagg Wood and the railway banking. After the next stile, the path veers away from the railway passing between two modern farm buildings to regain the road close to the level crossing.

Enjoy the mystic quality of this easy ramble amidst impressive limestone countryside where the influence of the little people is never far away.

6. Shake Hands with the Devil!

Mysteries:	Devil's Bridge, GR 616782. Fisherty Brow, GR 611789
Distance:	5½ miles
Total height climbed:	250 feet/76 metres
Nearest centre:	Kirkby Lonsdale
Start & finish:	Ample parking is available on the old road which forks left off the A65 down to Devil's Bridge.
Maps:	Ordnance Survey 1:25000, Pathfinder 628, Kirkby Lonsdale and Barbon.

Any walk that encompasses the beautifully rustic countryside around Kirkby Lonsdale cannot but include an exploration of this ancient settlement. Mentioned in the Domesday Book as *Cherchebi* meaning village with a church, it boasts an impressive pedigree stretching back to Roman times.

Picturesque and charming it certainly is being quaintly reminiscent of a nostalgic era when gentility and simple living were the norm. But nobody can accuse the town of being a preserved relic fit only for tourist voyeurs. Vibrant and active, the local community has managed to blend its antiquarian heritage into an amalgam for all to appreciate and enjoy.

Standing proud on top of an elevated site within a bend of the River Lune, Kirkby has been a focal point for fairs and markets since its charter was awarded in the 13th century. So it might come as something of a shock that such a romantic setting has been linked with devilish intrigue.

It has been said that no good ever came out of evil intent. Yet strung across the river lies the awesome result of just such a correlation. The Devil's Bridge has straddled the River Lune since at least 1365, when the local vicar was granted the right of *pontage* to collect tolls from travellers. Such moneys were then used to maintain the structure which was the sole means of gaining the far bank until 1932 when the 'modern' bridge was built.

No longer open to vehicular traffic, it is clear that only one carriage could negotiate the old bridge at a time owing to such a narrow span.

At one stage, historical writings tell us it was even more constricted with the pronouncement that 'two wheelbarrows trembled if they met'. Recessed alcoves enabled pedestrians to take refuge from the trundling carts.

Today, the old road provides ample parking from which to begin our walk. At the far side of the river, a first class kiosk has provided refreshment to visitors for many years. It is now a favourite meeting place for bikers from all over the North of England.

Exceptionally well populated on Bank Holidays when gladiators challenge the Devil at his own game by jumping from the parapet into the surging maelstrom below, it is also popular with scuba divers. Leaning over the middle of the three-ribbed arches, clearly *Old Scratch* still exerts a mesmeric effect on those who would scoff at his influence hereabouts.

Huge blocks of limestone tilt at ungainly angles where the massive supports of the primordial bridge soar upward from the swirling depths. Referred to as the *Devil's Neck Collar*, these grey boulders are reputed to have been dropped by the Prince of Darkness following the completion of his building project.

The Devil's Bridge, with the new road bridge beyond

The story is told of an old woman who arrived at the river crossing to fetch her cow for milking after it had strayed to the far side. Unfortunately by this time, the river was in full spate and impossible to cross. At that very moment, the Devil appeared.

"I will build you a new bridge," he said, "on condition that I take the soul of the first living thing to cross." The old woman agreed and returned home to await the morning.

Gathering stone from across Casterton Fell, the Devil laboured all night. As dawn appeared on the following day, a magnificent new bridge spanned the foaming torrent. Astonished at the Devil's accomplishment, the old woman was overjoyed and went to cross. Rubbing his hands at the prospect of a new recruit, 'Old Nick' proclaimed with gleeful anticipation, "Now you must carry out your part of the bargain."

"Certainly," announced the old woman hurling a small bun across to the far side of the bridge. "Fetch!" she called. Immediately, her dog ran across to retrieve the cake. "There!" she exclaimed in triumph. "You can have the soul of my dog."

As he fumed impotently at being cheated of his prey, the canny old dear crossed the bridge to collect her cow. With a howl of fury, the Devil threw himself from the bridge leaving a handprint as a lasting memorial to his thwarted ambition. The imprint can still be seen on the south side of the parapet. But should your hand fit exactly, do not be surprised to heed a sly cackle of suppressed laughter emanating from the brooding depths below.

The Walk

Go through the stile and make your way south along the right bank of the Lune soon crossing the main A65 road to continue. Take note of the new bridge and tranquil nature of the river's flow in contrast to the disturbance upstream amid the Devil's domain. This agreeable stroll follows an abandoned river terrace which indicates quite clearly the course it once followed.

Pass through a wall stile, followed by a gate after 300 metres, with the ruins of High Barn on the right. The route now adopts the terrace above the flood plain. It passes through a gate just beyond a bridge built to carry large pipes across the river. With rough tree growth along the river side, the path soon crosses a hedge stile followed immediately by

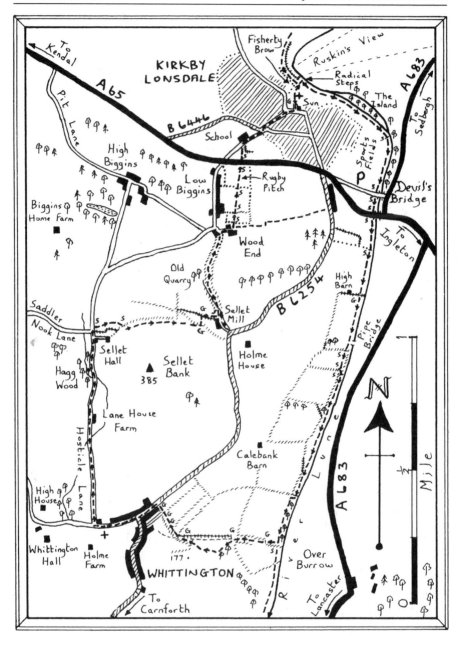

another to bring us back to the open river terrace. Widening out for almost half a mile, the hedge then veers back towards the river.

A further 100 metres and a fence stile is crossed, after which the path slants up to the elevated field again. At its end, leave the river path to push inland alongside a hedge. At the field corner, go through a gate to continue on the far side and down a short hedged corridor to another gate.

Here, an obvious track heads west towards the village of Whittington. The right-of-way, however, slants half left alongside an intermittent row of hawthorn trees. Pathless initially, it bears right to follow a grooved farm track around the edge of a knoll.

Leaning towards a hedge on the left, we soon cross the clear track and through a gate to mount a shallow rise. Passing through four more gates with a hedge on the left, we arrive at the secondary B6254 road on the outskirts of Whittington.

Turn left along the road for 200 metres keeping straight on up a side lane when the main road bends sharp left. The rough-cast stone church of St Michael the Archangel is erected on the site of a Saxon motte and bailey castle, although the present youthful structure only goes back to the 15th century.

Bear right up Hosticle Lane for about three-quarters of a mile to its junction with Saddler Nook Lane. A new stile on the right indicates an alteration to the original right-of-way. Sellet Hall, now used as an economic forestry research centre, is avoided completely. The new diversion descends an easy grass bank keeping right of a fence to rejoin the original route beyond a hedge stile.

Accompany this hedge down to a gate close to Sellet Mill. Cross the field and through another gate bearing right alongside a fence to the Mill hamlet. Turn left to pass behind a wooden structure along a path hemmed in by dense undergrowth.

This track follows an interesting if rather stony course that in part has been adopted by a tributary stream with its source in an old quarry. Making your way up the rough trail, watch out for a fallen tree where a deep bend of the thorax is required.

Above this section, the hedged track opens out and soon arrives at a metalled access road serving Wood End Farm. Bear right through the farm yard and take the signposted route across the fields to the *Grammar School*, now Queen Elizabeth's High School. Cross three fields through wall stiles, the final one being the school rugby pitch, to reach the A65 road.

Go straight across and continue ahead between fenced sporting courts to reach the road opposite the school entrance. Turn right towards the town centre forking left after 200 metres down Mitchelgate. Bear right at the bottom into Upper Market Street and then first left alongside the Sun Hotel to enter the grounds of St Mary the Virgin.

Note the wrought iron gateway and its unique spring mechanism on the side gates, simple yet ingenious. Pass left of this venerable Norman church, the focus of seven that comprise the parish of Kirkby Lonsdale known as *The Rainbow Churches* on account of the seven rainbow colours.

Head towards an Edwardian folly called The Gazebo beyond which is a natural hollow being an extension of the graveyard. This lies above the abrupt downfall of Fisherty Brow where it is said that an earlier church once stood. One Sunday during mass, a cataclysmic earthquake shook the ground and swallowed up the church together with the entire congregation. A report in 1883 claimed that every Sunday thereafter, the church bells were heard to ring summoning the souls of the departed.

Take a brief stroll down the elevated causeway above the Lune Valley there to admire the view. This scene so captivated the artist Turner that he felt compelled to put brush to canvas and record the idyllic landscape for posterity. So entranced was the celebrated painter that he urged his friend John Ruskin to pay a visit. This he did in 1875, saying that he could not recall another "place more naturally devine." *Ruskin's View* has altered little since. Merely to sit awhile absorbing the pastoral ambience of such a perfect setting can do more for the troubled soul than a pocketful of tranquillisers.

Returning to the aptly named Radical Steps, descend the steep stairway with the greatest of care. Once down at the river bank, turn right following a clear path alongside the Lune back to Devil's Bridge.

7. Hauntings Galore!

Mysteries:	Chase Corner, GR 101968; Muncaster Castle, GR 104963
Distance:	4½ miles
Total height climbed:	330 feet/100 metres
Nearest centre:	Ravenglass
Start & finish:	Free parking is available on the north side of the A595 opposite one of the entrances to Muncaster Castle grounds.
Maps:	Ordnance Survey English Lakes, 1:25000, south-west area sheet.

The Walk

Walk back up the main road towards Bootle. At the sharp bend known as Chase Corner, pause awhile in recollection of the grizzly occurrence that took place here almost a century ago. Until recently, there stood a large tree near this corner that was felled because of its danger to traffic. It marks the spot where a local woman was savagely put to death.

Mary Bragg lived in Ravenglass and was in love with a footman at the Muncaster Castle. Unknowingly, she had a jealous rival of some status who was the housekeeper there. This woman hired a coachman and groom to collect Mary from her home one day under the pretext that the footman was seriously ill and needed her attendance.

Driving along the main road, the coach drew to a halt under the first group of trees encountered at Chase Corner whereupon the groom shot Mary Bragg through the mouth. Her body was secretly buried in Hirst Plantation. Unfortunately for the perpetrators, it was soon discovered by a boy who immediately informed the Castle gardener. Swearing the lad to silence with the excuse that suspicion would hang over all the staff, the body was thrown into the River Esk where it was washed up days later down stream.

At the coroner's inquest, it was decided that the poor wretch had been drowned, severe disfigurement having been caused by frequent contact with the river bed and 'the chigling of eels'. Collusion by the doctors involved in the case was never proved even though suspicion of skulduggery was rife.

It might appear that justice had been severely lacking, but the guilty parties soon paid a heavy penalty for their nefarious sins. The house-keeper was ostracised from society, the groom went mad, and the coachman was hanged for highway robbery. All within a year of the atrocious crime. Mary cannot have been satisfied with this as she returned to haunt the grounds of Muncaster and became known as *The White Lady*. Even today, she is often to be seen darting across the road by passing motorists near to Chase Corner. One claims to have actually hit the spectre, but nothing was there when he stopped to assist. Locals refused to buy the timber cut from the infamous tree under which the murder took place.

The Tapestry Room, Muncaster Castle

Continue down the hill from Chase Corner turning right along the main access road serving the Castle. Constantly occupied by the Pennington Family since the 13th century, its turbulent history was been more than adequately documented elsewhere and is beyond the scope of this guide. Far more intriguing is the reputation it has acquired for being one of the most haunted residences in the country.

Skilled paranormal investigators from ASSAP (the Association for the Scientific Study of Anomalous Phenomena) have been unable to provide logical answers to the vexing aberrations that have plagued Muncaster for generations. Even the current owner has often sensed an unearthly presence that cannot be explained.

Many of the mysterious happenings have been blamed on *the Last Fool of Muncaster*. Tom Skelton was the castle jester back in the 16th century and possessed a streak of malicious intent that belied his jovial exterior. When guests displeased him, they were directed to cross the river estuary, where notorious quicksands could rapidly suck them under, instead of by the safe fording points nearby.

Thomas Skelton

Most heinous of the acts perpetrated by Tom Fool was condoned by the Lord of Muncaster himself who abhorred the fact that his betrothed daughter was smitten by the local carpenter. Waylaying the lovestruck fellow, the jester decapitated him and presented the gruesome trophy to his master. A spiteful quip at the craven deed put the word *tomfoolery* into the English language.

Since that time, a headless ghost is said to haunt the Tapestry Room where the brutal slaying took place, forever searching for his lost love. A futile task as the lady in question had retired to a Benedictine convent to assuage her broken heart.

Most prized of all the treasures within the Castle is *The Luck of Muncaster*. This bowl fashioned from Venetian glass was presented to Sir John Pennington by a grateful King Henry VI following defeat at the Battle of Hexham in 1463. After wandering alone for months, the fugitive was taken in and cared for by Sir John. A prayer accompanying the gift stated that the Penningtons would prosper as long as the *Luck* was intact and the family name survived. In the quixotic tongue of the day, "whyllys the famylie shold kepe hit unbrecken, they shold gretely thrif."

Take due time to assimilate the intoxicating atmosphere of this most enigmatic of stately homes, a sense of awe and mystery caressing you at every turn. Many are the unexplainable events that have persuaded the General Manager of the estate, Peter Frost-Pennington, that a night spent in the Tapestry Room is not one his priorities.

Once in the grounds, follow the succession of yellow-topped marker posts that indicate the right-of-way. After passing the estate office, cross the lawn where the fence on the right encloses the owl reserve. Affiliated to the World Owl Trust, the centre actively supports owl conservation on a global scale. These haunting creatures serve to enhance all that is mystical around Muncaster.

Should you wish to leave the right of way and enter the owl centre or explore the gardens and castle further, please buy a ticket first. These are available from within the Plant Centre or Gift Shop in the Stable Yard.

Merge with a major track and then fork right up a side trail after 50 metres into the woods. Climbing an easy gradient, the path soon reaches the edge of Dovecote Wood. Beyond a stile, a field opens up before you. Slant half left across the verdant sward down to a fence at the far side.

Over another stile, enter a sconce of conifers with a strange sunken building on the right. Roofless and overgrown, it used to be a water tank but has now been swallowed up by the encroaching woodland. What its original purpose was remains unclear. Drop down the narrow path between new plantings to reach the rough lane giving access to New-town.

Turn right between high banks of trees and stick with this wide track to the junction at Walls. Continue ahead for 200 metres in order to view the Roman Bath House. The red sandstone walls, all that remains of the important Glanaventa fort, convey a mood of history long since returned to nature. Vague images of sweat-stained centurions wallowing in the steam room might well be conjured up but only by applying a rampant imagination.

When the task becomes too much of a struggle, return to Walls and take the track down to the shore. Note that passage under the railway was designed for those who are vertically challenged. Should you forget this vital element, prepare to join the queue of headless spirits awaiting their turn to inhabit the Tapestry Room.

Once on the shore, head right along the shingle beach which is impassable only at the highest of tides. The steep bank was the site of the main fort of which there is no visible sign at present. Much of the site was ruined when the railway pushed right through the middle, the most recent of a series of communication facilities radiating out from Ravenglass.

Along the banks of the Esk estuary, a variety of gulls and terns breed in the low sand hills. Even the blind would be aware of their coastal situation from the salty tang and cawing of innumerable seabirds. Follow the shoreline round towards Ravenglass. Now silted up, this old fishing village was the first port to be established in West Cumbria.

Now one of the major attractions along this remote stretch of coast, the village has been saved from insignificance by *La'al Ratty*. The Ravenglass & Eskdale narrow gauge railway was initially developed in 1875 to carry haematite ore from Boot in Eskdale. Thereafter, the line became a passenger service and now carries a quarter million visitors each year.

Of singularly unique appeal, locomotives have found their way onto the Japanese miniature railway in Tokyo. For all who hanker nostalgi-cally after the great and glorious days of steam, the seven-mile trip up the beautiful Esk Valley is a must. If that is your bent, cross the mud flats to reach the main street of Ravenglass up a launching ramp. Take the first street on the right to cross the railway by a footbridge and so onto the station. If time is of the essence, head right before the first houses are reached. Pass through a gate and along a fenced path to another gate. Under the railway, it is but a brief stroll through the trees to the Walls access road.

Cross straight over into the opposite field and follow the fence on your left up to the next field. Take the gate on the left and make a diagonal crossing of this grassy pasture aiming for the wooded enclave ahead. The lone presence of a stone pillar indicates an ancient boundary.

Enter the wood by a stile and follow the thin trail through undergrowth to reach the main A595 road. A quarter of a mile to the east is the car park from where we started – but only for those who have protesting feet/or perhaps an urgent need to report the sighting of *The White Lady*. Others of a less cerebral disposition should head left down the road for 150 metres and take the rough lane on the right.

A gate is followed soon after by a stile and then the open fell is gained. Keep right of a fence to follow a clear track heading north up to another fence. Large clumps of prickly gorse on the right have made the stile redundant so pass through the gate as the path begins its descent to Barrow Plantation. Soon after the next fence stile, take a right fork to climb up through the tree cover. On your right, a new planting of conifers is being established.

When the gradient eases, the path makes a sharp right-hander at which point two other routes merge. Head south along the clear trail through a pass between rising tree clad banks. Ignore the right fork to Branken Wall which has been superseded by a permissive path soon joining the farm access track.

Cross straight over onto a clear track across the open field back to the car park. Though not an official right-of-way, your intrepid guide has obtained exclusive permission from the landowner permitting astute followers of this book to make use of it. At selected times of the year, due care should be exercised when the ancient sport of archery is practised hereabouts.

There can be no other locality where paranormal activity is so intense. Muncaster Castle fairly resonates with such unexplained phenomena, only adding to the splendid sense of antiquity to be felt here. But remember! Even such a noble personage as the late Lord Carlisle vowed never to remain a second night following his bizarre experience in the Tapestry Room. You have been warned.

8. Iron Mad in Lindale

Mystery: The Missing Coffin, GR 414804

Distance: 3½ miles

Total height climbed: 500 feet/152 metres

Nearest centre: Lindale

Start & finish: Park on the side of the B5277 secondary road about 100 metres after turning south towards Grange and adjacent to the Wilkinson Memorial.

Maps: Ordnance Survey 1:25000, Pathfinder 627 Milnthorpe, plus Pathfinder 636 Grange-over-Sands.

Nestling at the southern end of Newton Fell, a cluster of stone cottages occupies the land a little above the marshy tract to the east. Most of Lindale village swarms up the steepening lower reaches of Hampsfield Fell to avoid the flooding that used to occur before the construction of the embankment across the Winster estuary.

It was due to the endeavours of Lindale's most famous son, John Wilkinson, that the mossland was drained in the latter years of the 18th century before his death in 1805. The tall obelisk to his memory is tucked away on a raised natural platform and is often missed by people hurrying onward to the more prestigious resort of Grange-over-Sands some two miles down the road.

Made from cast iron plates now painted a deathly black, the monument pays tribute to one of the great pioneers of the Industrial Revolution. Most of Wilkinson's achievements were to increase the usage of iron products by considerably improving the manufacturing process.

He became known as *Iron Mad* Wilkinson due to his obsession with the ferrous ore, even building a cast iron chapel for the Methodists at the town of Bradley. Although most of his industrial empire was established in the Midlands, Wilkinson operated a furnace locally at Wilson House on the right of the B5277 a mile out of Lindale, where the products of his enterprise can still be seen. The great man himself lived in grand style at Castle Head in the lea of the rocky outcrop thrusting out of the flat mossland.

St Paul's Church

Once an important road junction, the village has now been by-passed. The gradual ascent of the new dual carriageway is far kinder to heavy lorries which used to wheeze and puff their way up the notorious Lindale Hill bound for Ulverston and Barrow. Winter freeze-ups were a common occurrence and caused problems on the hill when goods traffic often blocked the road.

It was at the time of field enclosures in the early 19th century that the village came to prominence as a focus of roads and local husbandry. First granted to the noble order of Knights Hospitaller in the 12th century, it came into the ownership of Hampsfield Hall in 1612.

The Walk

Cross the road and take the footpath to the right of the old police station. At the far right of the children's play area, go through a gate to emerge onto a narrow winding lane characteristic of this tiny settlement. Bear left past a cottage named Meadowcroft to mount some stone steps then passing through a stile. Climb the gently graded path beyond which soon brings you to a T-junction.

Go right circling round to arrive at the local primary school. The right-of-way passes through the playground marked out with an array of games of both ancient and modern vintage. Hopscotch is my favourite.

Turn left along the access lane climbing past a series of picturesque dwellings to arrive at St Paul's Church. Here on the right is located the final resting place of *Iron Mad* Wilkinson who lived up to his appendage by having an iron coffin built.

This was in fact the fifth time that the ironmaster had been buried. Slippage beneath the steeply canting cemetery has meant that the exact location of the unmarked grave is not known. The last person who could pin-point the site died some years ago, taking the bizarre mystery to his grave. Perhaps some enterprising parishioner could bring national recognition to Lindale with a metal detector.

Following his death at Bilston, John Wilkinson's heavy coffin was lost temporarily amid the sands whilst crossing Morecambe Bay. Later extricated, it was interred in a prepared plot at Castle Head. Unfortunately, the coffin was too small so a temporary plot was arranged until the new coffin was cast. Transfer to the new grave hit an unforeseen problem in the form of solid rock, making it too shallow.

Eventually, the master of Castle Head found peace, but only for twenty years. The new owners objected to the grave and its iron memorial thus requiring its disinterment yet again. Both finally made it to their current sites. Although it appears that the spirit of the *Iron King* has taken revenge for his shoddy treatment and is no doubt chuckling gleefully at the mystery he has inadvertently created.

After speculating as to his whereabouts, leave the graveyard and continue up to the B5271. Turn left followed by a right up Lingarth. At the end of the cul-de-sac, join a track followed by stone steps passing through a stile. Accompany the wall uphill to cross the private road serving Hampsfield.

Drop down through a stile making your way to the far side of a field and another stile before crossing to the old settlement of Hampsfield Farm. Now renamed as Holme Farm (right) and Stonegarth (left), turn left up a short walled track. Pass through the gate and walk along the wall to a stile there to enter enclosed woodland.

Slant right along a clearly 'rooted' trail down to a gate. This will bring you to the eastern limit of Tithe Allotment. Follow the outer edge of the wood to the next gate and re-enter Eggerslack Wood.

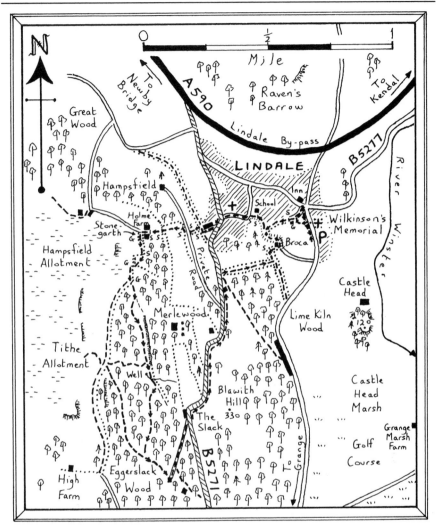

Swing right along a good path and then left down a dry valley with a low scar on the left. As height is lost, watch out for uprooted trees that will test your skill as a contortionist. Just beyond a spring, the original right-of-way has to be abandoned as it mysteriously enters private grounds. Is this a re-routing which the Ordnance Survey is not privy to?

Err on the side of discretion by veering right and then left to join the main path descending from Hampsfield Fell. Soon thereafter, turn left down a metalled right-of-way to emerge onto the B5271 close to The Slack.

Head north past this group of dwellings followed after a quarter of a mile by the entrance to Merlewood, the ecology research establishment. After another quarter mile, keep watch for a clear sign on the right where two footpaths descend on either side of Little Kiln Wood.

Take the left path down a narrow walled track to a T-junction at the bottom. Bear left again and follow this path round to the access road serving Broca. Pass to the right of the house where the rough track continues on towards Lindale primary school.

Watch for the right turn down the outward route which brings us back to Meadowcroft. As an alternative, stick with this back lane which emerges at the bottom of Lindale Hill opposite the Inn where refreshment for all persuasions is on tap. A brief stroll back along the Grange road will return you safely to the Wilkinson Memorial.

9. Dance with the Devil

Mystery: The Wizard of Murthwaite, GR 514007

Distance: 5 miles

Total height climbed: 475 feet/145 metres

Nearest centre: Burneside

Start & finish: Park on the left-hand grass verge immediately south of Garnett Bridge on the Potter Fell Road.

Maps: Ordnance Survey English Lakes, 1:25000, south-east area sheet.

Unobtrusively remote from the main arteries serving Lakeland, the valleys of the south-east have changed but little over the centuries. Refurbishment of cottage interiors and a tarmacadam road are the only concessions surrendered to the modern world. None of these dales allow through traffic, a feature that has saved them from unwarranted exploitation.

Thankfully, a proposal to link the neighbouring valleys of Kentmere and Longsleddale over Green Quarter Fell never came to fruition. A circular route would have destroyed the natural seclusion of both dales forever. Only locals and discerning fell wanderers bother to make the protracted journey up the narrow access road.

Expansion of Haweswater into a reservoir for Manchester certainly had its repercussions in Longsleddale, the only visible evidence of such being a series of survey posts used in the construction of the pipe line. The inherent peace of the valley was disturbed for a time by the pipe-laying gangs, many of whom took lodgings in local farms. Indeed, Murthwaite bears the scars of a fire started after a fateful night's carousing.

A second tunnel under Gatescarth Pass was abandoned in mid-century following fierce opposition by residents, enabling the valley to settle back into its leisurely pace again.

Divided into two distinct geological constituents, the southern element where this walk takes place presents the subdued appearance characteristic of Silurian Slates. Though still assuming the classic shape associated with glacial erosion, a softening of the landscape makes for easy walking terrain. Once Sadgill is reached, the raw nature of the landscape alters dramatically with exposed cliffs of splintered rock rearing up on either side of the dale head.

The Walk

Our walk begins at Garnett Bridge where the River Sprint pulsates through a narrow rock strewn gorge. The hamlet grew to prominence because of this surging torrent which powered bobbin, corn and woollen mills. Once a bustling settlement, nothing has outwardly changed since the mill wheels ceased their onerous chore.

Take a stroll down past Riverside Guesthouse and back towards the bridge. Fork left along a walled track which once connected all the farms on this side of the valley. Now superseded as the main line of communication, it still provides a first rate path for walkers.

Beyond the first gate, the route follows a hedge on the right. Slanting round to the left, a rough walled lane is reached which connects with Cocks Close. Here, we pass through a pair of gates and mount the facing grass bank to reach the opposite corner of the field.

Enter the next field through a gate and head north-west with a wall on the right. Continue ahead in a direct line crossing to the opposite side of the wall at the field boundary and another gate. The track now approaches a bend in the Sprint close to a small copse of trees and merges with the access track serving Nether House Farm.

The right-of-way passes right of the farm buildings and carries on past a set of upright slate piles. Across the other side of the river lies Murthwaite, the focus of our mystery on this walk. Pass the next settlement of Tenter Howe and so on to Bridge End.

A newly erected stone bungalow contrasts sharply with the old farm cottage on the opposite side of the track. After passing through the first gate, leave the obvious track to enter a level field whilst enjoying the placid calm that remains an inherent feature that has drawn me back to Longsleddale time and again. Go through the gate at the far side and over a spindly gill to join the access road serving Docker Nook. Turn right to reach the main valley road.

From here, the rugged grandeur personified in Borrowdale Volcanic terrain beyond Sadgill fills the northern prospect. In contrast to this bold facade, our walk is restricted to the sleek flanks of the lower valley.

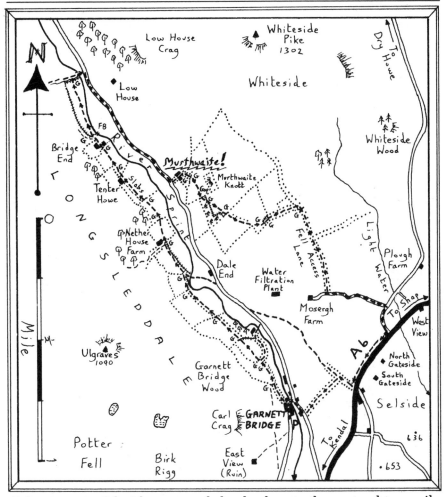

Sylvan tracts of deciduous woods lend colour to the pastoral tranquillity in timeless embodiment.

An astute guide book writer of the last century, M.J.B. Baddeley, stated that "it is difficult to picture a scene in which peace, contentment and beauty are more happily combined." Thankfully, his observations are still pertinent today, and hopefully always will be.

Stroll back towards Garnett Bridge past Low House marvelling at the lofty valley sides which soar up proud and aloof. At Murthwaite, turn left into the farmyard, home of the infamous *Wizard of Longsleddale* who practised his iniquitous talents here during the 17th century.

Murthwaite Farm

Dr Lickbarrow is reputed to have dabbled in the black arts whilst maintaining an outward display of piety as a regular churchgoer.

On one occasion whilst attending the local church up the valley, a violent storm blew up. Slates were torn from the roof and tree branches snapped like match wood pummelling the tiny structure. Realising that mischief from the devil's hand was afoot, he hurried back to Murthwaite. A servant met him at the gate with the news that all manner of inexplicable happenings had taken place.

On hearing this, the doctor burst into his living room to find a young apprentice perusing his *Book of Magic*. Propped open at the chapter headed *How to raise the Devil*, it was clear how the roguery had been stirred up. Once opened, Old Nick had wasted no time. After throwing the petrified youth from the room, Lickbarrow struggled mightily to close the potent tome. No easy task even for one with his mastery of the craft, but eventually the mayhem was contained.

In those times of rampant superstition, the powers associated with the enigmatic doctor were treated with respectful amazement. Many were the surreptitious callers requiring help to recover lost goods, or seeking cures for their ailments. Like many of his contemporaries,

Lickbarrow's quack remedies took little heed of accepted medical practice. Nevertheless, his reputation among the simple folk of the valley continued to flourish.

Even as the end drew nigh, the doctor still sustained an interest in the unearthly. Lying close to death, two pigeons were seen fighting on the roof of Murthwaite. When informed that the black one had defeated its white adversary, he muttered, "Its all over with me, then!" Soon after, he slipped into the next life.

In the living room of the farmhouse is to be found an old cupboard set in the thick stone wall. Carved into the hard wood is the date 1679 with the initials *I E L* above. Could this have been home to the dreaded *Book of Magic*? Certainly today the house has thrown off the devil's scarf that once embraced its stolid portals. Holiday accommodation dispensed with Cumbrian hospitality now make it an ideal retreat for visitors to this remote outback.

Pass through the gate close to the house and enter a short walled access passage to the open fell above. Climbing the steep fell side above Murthwaite, the angled path provides an easy gradient. A gap in the next fell wall leads into the edge of a new conifer planting. Immediately after, pass through a fence gate to continue up the track above the plantation.

Locate the gate through the next wall at the top edge of the tree cover which is here fenced off. As the apex of the ridge is approached, keep right of an intermittent broken wall. On reaching a wall corner, bear half left across the upper pasture to a small fenced enclosure. The elevated skyline ahead is the Whinfell ridge where twin radio masts intrude on an otherwise sublime horizon.

Beyond a gate, take a stroll along a walled corridor to join the fell access lane. Local farmers have long used this enclosed highway to drive their flocks up to the rough grazing above the in-take walls. Turn right and descend the elongated track until a T-junction is reached.

This paved road serves Mosergh Farm to the right. Our way lies left down to another T-junction; take a right turn here to arrive at the main A6 road. Head right towards Kendal for no more than half a mile, until a walled path is reached on the right opposite a back lane and some buildings. Great care must be exercised on this brief section of road as no pavement is provided and the grass verge is extremely narrow.

Turn right along this short cut to Longsleddale for walkers. After 100 metres, bear left down a steepening passage. Walled and constricted, it acts as an escape channel for water after heavy rain which can turn the ground into a mud slick.

On gaining the valley road, swing right down to Garnett Bridge. Perched above the bubbling cauldron of the Sprint as it elbows out of the bottle neck, it becomes clear why the hamlet emerged as a focus of rural industry when water power was supreme.

Dropping out of the 20th century is a simple matter of veering left off the Shap road down into Longsleddale. Beyond the confines of the valley, science and technology provide all the answers to our dilemmas. But not everything can be explained in so logical a manner. Many people still elicit a sympathetic accord with the ancient legends that remain a spirited ingredient of local heritage.

Nobody ever did find Dr Lickbarrow's *Book of Magic* after his death.

10. Levens Hall

Mysteries:	The Grey Lady, GR 496852. The Luck of Levens, GR 5085
Distance:	4½ miles
Total height climbed:	430 feet/131 metres
Nearest centre:	Sedgwick
Start & finish:	Park in the lay-by on the old A6 just beyond the sharp left-hander after crossing Levens Bridge.
Maps:	Ordnance Survey 1:25000 Pathfinder 627, Milnthorpe sheet.

Located close to the last stage of the ageing River Kent before it enters Morecambe Bay, Levens Hall lies some distance from the village that bears its name. Dating back to 1188, the current main house was built towards the end of the first Elizabethan era.

Topiary, the art of hedge and tree design, has brought international acclaim to the Hall. Fortunate indeed were the owners to have acquired the commendable expertise of landscaper Monsieur Guillaume Beaumont, who began his long term project of laying out the gardens in 1689. Fashions come and go but the essential design as created by the French gardener has survived unchanged and includes many rare plants not found elsewhere.

Stylishly pruned trees of beech, box and yew peep over the outer wall as you approach the well known river-crossing point at Levens Bridge. Make time to visit the impressively fortified house and wander freely about this unique setting. A more romantic locale you would be hard pressed to find.

With continuous residence for several centuries, it is little wonder that Levens Hall has acquired its own peculiar array of singular occurrences. Beware of the black dog should you visit the house alone. He is known to dash in front of visitors almost tripping them up and then disappearing without trace.

More sinister, however, is the ghost of *The Grey Lady* who has frequently been seen distracting motorists on the road outside the Hall. Thought to be a gypsy who was refused food and shelter by the Lord of the Manor early in the 18th century, she subsequently died of starvation. Laying a curse on the family before passing away, she prophesied that no son would be born to inherit the estate until the Kent ceased to flow and a white a fawn was born within the herd of black fallow deer that roam Levens Park.

Years passed with the curse firmly entrenched. Not until 1896 was a son finally born to the Lady of the House and then only after a white fawn had appeared. What effectively buried the curse was that in the same year, the River Kent did in fact cease to flow by completely freezing over. The Grey Lady still makes occasional appearances, often accompanied by a *black dog*!

"Luck to Levens while the Kent flows" is a traditional toast offered by guests whilst imbibing the renowned Morocco Ale brewed at the Hall. Matured for twenty-one years, its potency is said to be without equal. One wonders whether The Grey Lady appears to those who have quaffed a dram too many.

Emblazoned on the coat of arms are three pillows which are known to relate to a particularly laid back member of the Redmayne Family who was challenged to a duel. His arrival at the appointed site being rather early, he elected to take a brief repose in a nearby tent. He

Levens Hall

promptly fell asleep only to be rudely awakened by a flurry of trumpets heralding the start of the contest.

Grabbing his sword, the tardy knight dashed forth. Much to the surprise of the gathered assemblage, he slew his adversary before the bemused fellow had time to recover his composure. Our somnolent hero must have been defending the honour of the Redmaynes to have had such a quirky exploit immortalised on the family shield.

The Walk

Our walk starts by crossing the River Kent by way of Levens Bridge and taking a left through a small gate in the wall to enter the planned woodland of Levens Park. Hugging both sides of the river for a mile up to the cataract of Park Head Falls, our route follows the right bank. Once described as "the sweetest spot that fancy can imagine", the park was also laid out by Guillaume Beaumont. It was, however, substantially reduced in size following the destruction of seven hundred trees in a storm.

Black Fallow Deer arrived at Levens around 1600 and although shy creatures, are easily spotted in the narrow confines of the park. It is said that whenever a white fawn is born, some momentous event of change takes place affecting Levens Hall. Eminent births, deaths and marriages have occurred to support this story. Known as *The Luck of Levens*, ill fortunes will dog the house should any of these white deer be slain deliberately.

One gamekeeper was ordered to shoot a white deer to preserve the dark strain in the herd. Appalled by the insensitive manner exhibited by Lord Templeton, who was the current owner, he refused outright. Not to be usurped by an underling, Lord Templeton instructed another servant to carry out the foul deed. Henceforth for some considerable time, a panoply of disasters befell the residents in quick succession.

Now follow the path in a general easterly direction with the river on your left. Following a gradual ascent away from the river, the path joins the long avenue of oaks which forms the main focus of the park like a majestic guard of honour. At the end, bear right through another small gate to arrive at a back lane.

Turn left towards Sedgwick and over the main motorway access road, then immediately right up a flight of steps. A stile takes you to the Lancaster Canal. Now abandoned and filled in, it is completely unrec-

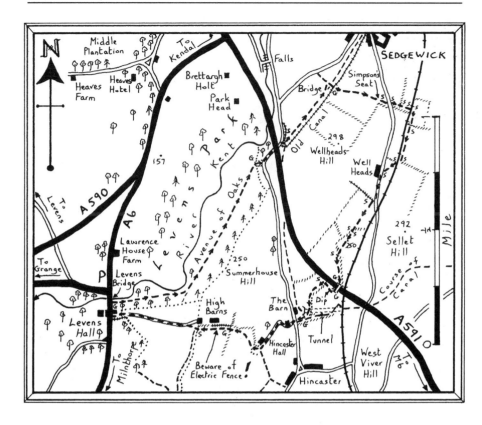

ognisable as such. Follow a thin path which accompanies a fence towards the north-west along the course of this once thriving waterway.

Cross the next bridge, which has become isolated in a sea of grass, and pass through a gate. Our route lies across the field up a pathless grass slope. This is the only section of the walk that involves anything like a climb, and Simpson's Seat erected in 1994 provides a brief recovery from your exertions. Located at the corner of a hedge, it faces due north where the view is dominated by the Neolithic hill fort of the Helm.

Drop down the far side of the hill through a stile to cross a lane and through another stile to mount the short facing rise. Another hedge stile and descent will bring you to the main west coast railway line, here crossed with customary care and attention. Bear right alongside the fenced track on your right. Cross a stile and continue along the line to the field end where we must cross back to the west side of the railway.

A stile to cross the track-side fence is followed immediately by a wall stile. Thereafter, a diagonal stroll to the far side of the field and we meet up with the back road at Well Heads. Head south for 200 metres before entering a field by way of a stile. Mount the tail of a regular drumlin aiming for a double stile in the hedge/fence ahead.

Then maintain a south-west bearing across the apex of the drumlin noting the slant of the railway as it picks a course between the mounds. A more detailed analysis of these geomorphic phenomena is to be found in Walk 2.

With a hedge on your right, aim for the mid-point of the facing hedge to pass over a stile. The original right-of-way continued straight ahead but has now been abandoned due to its dissection by the motorway link road. Instead therefore, slant left along the hedge down to a farm bridge gated at either end. Cross the road and lean immediately right past a sheep dipping pen. Follow the road back for 100 metres to cross a hedge stile then bend left alongside this over a brow.

Curve down to the left as the field boundary becomes walled. Take note of the Lancaster Canal exit on the left from the Hincaster Tunnel. Cutting through the hill for 345 metres, the tunnel did not have a towpath for the horses which were led across to rejoin the canal close to a house called The Barn.

Completed in 1817, primarily to serve the Wakefield Gunpowder Company based at Sedgwick, it was constructed from four million bricks. Clay for these was dug locally at Moss Farm and carted to the site where the bricks were made. Parts of the tunnel built under water were lined with limestone due to its porous quality to prevent flooding.

At this point, the canal bed is still visible but overgrown with vegetation. We join the road to the north of Hincaster village, next to this path.

Cross straight over and head down the access road serving Hincaster Hall. After passing the hall on your right, the path becomes rough as it bends round to the right through a gate. The open track then arcs to the left homing in to a hedge on the right and dropping down to a gate.

Beyond this, the farm outbuildings of High Barns must be passed on your right. What should be a simple task is hindered by the positioning of an electric fence across the right-of-way. Doubtless to prevent animals from straying, this obtrusive hazard still has to be negotiated if progress back to Levens Hall is to be continued. Your task is to manage this with dignity and in safety and so reach the wall abutting the farmhouse. Beyond the wall, join the farm access road to cross the large field back to the main road opposite the entrance to the Hall.

Once again, one of these mysterious walks pays tribute to an old residence of unquestionable charm and charisma from which has emerged a picturesque heritage to complement the hardware. Reality and legend sit comfortably at Levens. But no amount of dialogue can replace the experience of taking a stroll around these fascinating grounds to absorb the ambient mood of centuries. But mind you, don't trip over that abrasive hound!

11. Ghosts and Dobbies

Mysteries:	Hawes Bridge, GR 512891. Sizergh Castle, GR 498879
Distance:	6 miles
Total height climbed:	370 feet/113 metres
Nearest centre:	Natland
Start & finish:	There is ample parking space near the Strickland Arms on the old section of the A6 that has now been by-passed.
Maps:	Ordnance Survey Pathfinder Series 627 1:25,000 Milnthorpe sheet.

With tales of ghosts and dobbies abounding throughout the Lake Counties, it will come as no surprise that two such occurrences are met on this walk. Indeed, the Kent Valley is fortunate in possessing one of the few places in England where recalcitrant spirits can be confined after their exorcism. (Non-Cumbrians please note: a 'dobbie' is a gregarious and friendly spirit, quite unlike the unpleasant and humourless 'boggles' encountered elsewhere in this book!)

Hawes Bridge is unique in this respect according to the psychic sages of Westmorland. As such, this expedition should not be entered into lightly nor approaching the twilight hours when creatures from the "other side" are at their most spiteful.

The Walk

With this in mind, take the side road branching right away from the Strickland Arms (named after the local family associated with Sizergh Castle) to pass under the new road. Follow this narrow lane down to the banks of the River Kent and there head left alongside the river towards Low Park Caravan Site. Cross the footbridge suspended above the broad spate to reach the far side just north of Wilson's Place.

Head upstream along the tree-girt watercourse on a grass track that passes through a gate at the narrowest part of Larkrigg Spring. At this point the river is concealed by thick tree growth. Continuing along the track, it soon veers away from the river making a sharp right before passing through a gate. Make a diagonal crossing of the field and aim

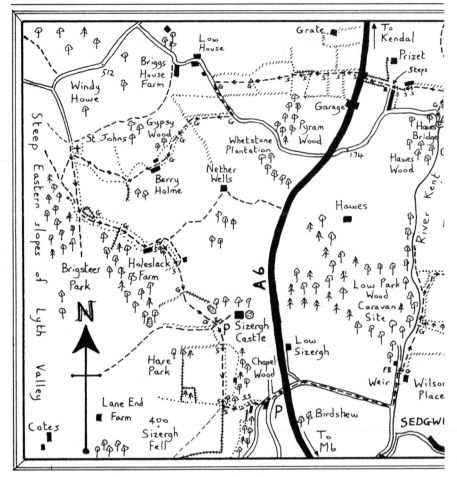

for the raised embankment ahead. A stile provides access onto the towpath of what used to be the Lancaster Canal.

This stretch has now been abandoned with much of its length up to Kendal having been filled in. Once a vital artery for the transit of goods between Preston and Kendal, the waterway terminates abruptly just south of Stainton at GR 531854. Where we join it at Larkrigg Hall Bridge, the depth and overall dimensions of the original construction are still visible. Too soon as we head north along the towpath, the canal has been filled in and given over to sheep and cattle pasture.

Two stiles need to be crossed where fields have been extended before Crowpark Bridge is reached. This stone structure now appears as an

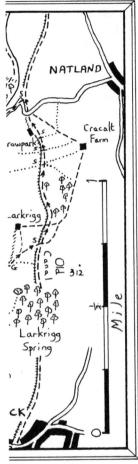

ancient and redundant relic from our past industrial heritage. Just beyond the bridge, leave the towp.1th by way of a stile and descend the meandering lane into the enclosed sylvan recess of the Kent Valley.

Hawes Bridge offers passage across the ravine. Here, the swirling river is squeezed between layered beds of fluted limestone. It is indeed an eerie locale. Known to have interred dobbies which had caused ill luck nearby, their spirits were chained to the supports beneath the bridge. According to primeval laws of the nether world, such denizens would appear only to one person at a time.

When perceived with the human eye, the ghostly inmate was unable to vent any form of utterance, which is perhaps just as well else much outpouring of bleep rated expletives would doubtless have followed. Likewise, should assaults on the ear be made, dobbies remained invisible, the exception being if they were addressed in the name of God. All spirits are like to tremble with fear when challenged before their Maker. Ensure, therefore, that your travels in the neighbourhood of Hawes Bridge are not after dusk, when they are at their most malevolent.

Take due heed of this spectral site before continuing across the bridge and up the road. After only fifty metres at the sharp left-hander, go through the gate on your right. At this point, walkers like myself with old maps may be tempted to cross the field directly to Prizet being unaware of the changing course of the right-of-way. Instead, continue along the path by the river up to the next gate but do not go through. Bear left and follow the field edge uphill crossing two stiles before entering a channelled pathway. Wooden steps thence bring you onto the access road serving Prizet Hall.

Cross straight over along a broad fenced corridor to reach the main A6 road adjacent to the estate lodge. Great care must be exercised when negotiating this busy dual-carriageway if the walk is to be completed unscathed. Nobody has any desire to cross swords with the captive entities secreted under Hawes Bridge before due time.

At the far side, continue heading due east alongside the hedge boundaries of four fields. The following two fields are then crossed mid-way to reach the back lane, which winds up onto the limestone ridge bounding the Lyth Valley. Keep left for 300 metres, watching for a gate on the right which points the way east again – but with no signpost.

Initially, the right-of-way accompanies a wall and later a hedge before slanting left towards a gate at the far side of the field. Thereafter, head south-west alongside another wall on your left. Now a clear trail, it passes right of a copse and then between a new barn and the old stone edifice of Berry Holme.

Join the paved farm access road at its far side which breaks close to the church of St John. Remote from any village, the church offers spiritual guidance for a scattered congregation drawn from isolated settlements in the parish of Helsington. Go in and sign the visitors' book; a welcome retreat from bad weather, or lost dobbies.

Few other churches can enjoy such a regal and elevated position above the flat bottom-land of the Lyth Valley. The drained tracts of marshy ground astride the River Gilpin and broken by rocky knolls of limestone are far removed from the scabrous heartland of the District, but no less attractive for that. High Heads and Gilpin Bank were once islands when the valley was inundated by the sea.

On the far side, the massed ranks of coniferous trees which cloak the slopes of Whitbarrow Scar once extended unbroken to the shores of Lake Windermere. In days of yesteryear, wild boar roamed the forests unchecked. One such truculent specimen wreaked havoc amongst the valley settlers killing farm animals and even attacking the residents. It was only due to the gallant bravery of Richard de Gylpin that the savage beast was eventually tracked to its lair and slain.

Here, on the open grassy flanks of Windy Howe, model aircraft enthusiasts meet regularly to practise remote control techniques. A seat in front of the church makes a prime viewpoint overlooking the entrance to this fine secluded valley where the ageing Rivers Kent and Gilpin converge to feed into Morecambe Bay.

Head south along a rough track, open on the valley flank with a wall on your left. When the track enters woodland, it leans to the left through a gate and then descends a coarse gradient. It emerges into the yard of

Holeslack Farm, an ancient homestead with the circular chimneys characteristic of Elizabethan architecture.

Just beyond the farm buildings, watch for a wooden stile on the right after which, the path enters a dense clutch of undergrowth and the nearest you are likely to come to a jungle trek. Thorny tendrils of shrubbery struggle to hinder progress at every turn. An exciting trod for intrepid adventurers only. But too soon, the exit stile is reached.

Those of an easy-going disposition should stick to the main track which is joined close to a barn. Half a mile to the south-east, the crenellated battlements of Sizergh Castle can just be discerned above the surrounding sconce of trees. Cross the field and thence through a gate and across another field. This emerges onto the main access track between Sizergh and the Lyth Valley close to a fenced dog walking pound. Facing you is the large car park serving the castle.

Turn left to inspect the inner sanctum of this most illustrious of Lakeland houses. Even if a tour is not on your itinerary, do not miss this opportunity to view the grounds, especially the rock garden designed by Lady Strickland in 1926.

Sizergh Castle

Although Sizergh itself can be traced back to Norse times when a settler named Sigrith established a dairy farm here, the present building dates back to 1340. The huge pele tower being the largest in Cumbria is the centre piece. With walls 58 feet (18 metres) high and averaging 7 feet (2 metres) thick, this dour blockhouse was constructed to withstand the ravaging onslaught of Celtic brigands sweeping down from north of the border. Not until 1450 was the Great Hall tacked onto the tower to be enlarged by Sir Walter Strickland in the following century.

Twenty-seven generations of the Strickland family were the sole incumbents of Sizergh Castle from 1239 until it passed into the hands of the National Trust in 1950. Before this, the estate was granted to Gervase Deincourt by Henry II in 1170.

Reputed to be a fierce and lusty warrior-baron, it is said that he was an insanely jealous man who distrusted his young wife even though he loved her with a fervent passion. When summoned by the king to fight the marauding Scots, Gervase locked his wife away and threatened the servants with death if they released her. So terrified were they, that the poor woman was completely ignored causing her to suffer the ghastly torment of slow starvation.

No one is quite sure which was the infamous locked room, but the lady's ghost still walks the silent corridors of Sizergh emitting a dreadful wail of anguish to be released from her eternal plight.

To leave Sizergh, follow the right edge of the car park along a hedge until a stile is reached. Walk the length of the next field with a wall on your left. At its far end, cross a fence stile followed immediately by another on the left. Accompany the southern wall limit of Chapel Wood down a steepening grass bank. Keep to this pathless left side to avoid private allotments lower down. Cross two stiles near the bottom to emerge onto the back lane from Levens village close to a row of cottages.

Walk down the back lane to the Strickland Arms and some welcome lubrication of the tonsils to exorcise the remnants of any dobbies that might have tagged along.

open terrain. Lonely indeed is the grazing land between Troutbeck and Kentmere where few walkers will be encountered.

On this particular occasion, an absolute silence enfolded the Common. Not a single breath of wind disturbed the tough moorland grasses. Only the faint bleating of new born lambs persuaded me that other creatures were abroad on this placid day.

Such quietude might well stimulate the imagination to play tricks with one's mind. But I really did experience a certain presence following behind me along the grassy trod. On more than one occasion, I distinctly heard steps behind me, but on turning round, the path was deserted. I even peered over the wall. Nothing.

Maybe the souls of long forgotten travellers still wander these fell trails and in rare circumstances, break through that fine barrier separating past from present. A fascinating mystery to contemplate whilst heading north across the plateau of Mickle Moss towards Sallows.

After passing through the third gate beyond Mickle Moss, the path slants away from the fell walls as the shallow upper valley of Park Beck

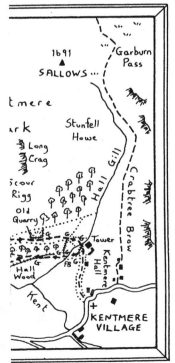

is neared. Cross the ford abutting a sheepfold at a point where the path accompanies the final in-take wall around the elongated east shoulder of Sallows known as Whiteside End.

The grassy nature of the path becomes exceedingly stony on the gradual descent to Kentmere Hall. This is the main access track for farm vehicles bound for the open fell of Kentmere Park. After passing an old abandoned stone quarry, the heart quickens and the pulse races as our main objective comes into view.

Kentmere Hall with its antiquarian pele tower has witnessed many strange happenings during its chequered history. But none so quirky as that involving the "Cork Lad of Kentmere".

Born the son of a monk from Furness Abbey, Hugh Hird arrived in Kentmere with his disgraced mother during the reign of Edward VI. Employed by the De Gilpins of Kentmere Hall because of his enormous strength, it was

Hugh who single-handedly lifted the ten metre kitchen beam into position. This was during the addition of the present main structure built onto the pele tower, and after several local lads had struggled in vain with the prodigious task.

Summoned to attend the court of King Edward in London, the giant endeared himself to the Crown by performing spectacular feats of strength. His mammoth appetite was no less impressive either. A whole sheep washed down with copious flagons of wine was a mere snack to the 'Cork Lad'.

When asked what gift he would most desire, the giant requested the rightful use of a small tenement with a stand of timber for fuel. Hird Wood and an old house named after him can still be found to the west of The Tongue alongside Trout Beck. Hugh spent the rest of his life in the Troutbeck Valley moving colossal boulders and uprooting trees. It was this latter exertion that finally sent the hapless fellow to meet his maker.

A working farm, Kentmere Hall supports upwards of 1300 Swaledale ewes and 75 cows on 125 acres of in-bye land with grazing rights on the open fell. It remains much as it was in Hugh Hird's day. Once the

Kentmere Hall – defensive pele tower

threat from plundering Scots had diminished, the old tower was finally abandoned in favour of permanent residency in the new farmhouse. Today it affords an engaging link with a turbulent past that has no equal in today's Lakeland.

The right-of-way makes a U-turn in front of the hall to head south at valley level. Immediately beyond the second gate, cross Hall Gill on a newly constructed footbridge. After entering Hall Wood, watch for a fork in the clear trail. Take the left arm to follow the lower beat which leaves the sylvan cloak opposite the northern limit of Kentmere Tarn.

Hugh Hird would have been shocked to observe the diminution of this once sublime expanse. Evidence of the size to which it once espoused can be pictured from the extent of the reed beds. Described in 1577 as "*a poole a myle compass*", the lake was drained around 1850 to deliver more land for pasturage and cultivation.

Two ancient dugout canoes and a Viking spear were found, offering evidence of a much earlier settlement of the valley than was previously recognised. Far more significant, however, regarding the future development of Kentmere was the discovery of diatomite. With insulating properties able to withstand high temperatures, the works set up to exploit this valuable material is still in operation and furnishes much needed local employment.

As the tarn is unseen from the valley road, Kentmere is generally regarded as a '*dry valley*' even though it is slowly re-establishing itself. Fishing is now the principal activity and a lower path parallels our route allowing access for licensed anglers. Continue along this old highway, once a major thoroughfare on the west side of the valley. Now confined to walkers, it is nevertheless a joy to promenade.

After passing through the yard of the diatomite works operated by Hepworth industries, take the metalled access road to Sawmill Cottage which is now a local craft centre. The right-of-way is chaperoned across a well-kept lawn by a narrow strip steel fence. Cross the footbridge at the bottom end of the garden to pass behind a sconce of bushes. Emerging into a grassy walled lane, it is but 100 metres to a T-junction where we turn left past Croft Head to return from whence we came over Ulthwaite Bridge.

Enjoy this opportunity to journey back in time and visit the Kentmere of the 'Cork Lad' whose legendary strength has never been surpassed.

13. Disturbance in Dunnerdale

Mysteries:	The Mighty Salmon, GR 213954. The Newfield Riot, GR 227960
Distance:	4 miles
Total height climbed:	460 feet/140 metres, including Wallowbarrow at 630 feet/192 metres
Nearest centre:	Seathwaite
Start & finish:	A small car park on the left just north of Seathwaite Church.
Maps:	Ordnance Survey 1:25000, English Lakes, south-west area sheet.

Secluded and remote, Dunnerdale does not display that essential stark excitement that has become the hall mark of classic Lakeland scenery. This is greatly to its advantage for in consequence it receives fewer visitors. Those who do venture along the tortuous narrow road between Wrynose Bottom and the Duddon Sands can savour the sheer joy of sampling Lakeland at its best.

In its upper reaches, the River Duddon squeezes between tree clad flanks which culminate in the awesome cleft of Wallowbarrow Gorge. Thereafter, the river swings in a series of wide loops across the flat valley floor whose configuration is more in keeping with how one would expect a glacial valley to appear. Not willing to be cast in such a conformist mould, the river is again pinched between the jaws of Duddon Bridge and Bank End before escaping across the open salt marsh estuary to the sea.

The eminent poet and writer, Norman Nicholson who came from nearby Millom, preferred to visit the dale in late autumn when the midday sun poured down the valley reducing shadows to a minimum. For me, Dunnerdale will always present its true colours in spring time when a broad scattering of lavender bluebells in the woods and on the lower fellside contrasts with the rusty hue of dead bracken.

Approaching from the south, entry into the dale is from above, after which the road drops down to the valley floor. Beyond Ulpha, the first hamlet is Hall Dunnerdale, an ancient cluster of cottages and farms

Scratched outline of the Dawson salmon at Hall Dunnerdale

where the largest salmon ever seen in Lakeland was hooked from the churning river back in 1936.

To preserve this momentous catch so none could doubt his claim, James Dawson, a local garage proprietor and bicycle repairer, laid the magnificent specimen on a concrete slab in front of his house near to Hall Bridge. Clutching a six-inch nail, he carved an outline around the 26lb (12kg) monster and posed for numerous photographs.

These are still in the possession of his sisters, unlike the fish which was no doubt consumed with relish by the Dawson family. Such was its size that plenty would have remained for the rest of the village to enjoy.

After due deliberation of this unique happening, continue up the valley to the village of Seathwaite where occurred an event one July day in 1904 the gravity of which cannot be over stated. In the annals of local history, this was *Black Monday* which began like any other pay-day and ended with one man shot dead and another desperately wounded.

Trouble flared between Irish navvies building a reservoir above Seathwaite, and other workers who had trekked over from Haverigg to carry on their carousing at the Newfield Inn. After being thrown out of the pub for causing excessive damage, the incensed mob laid siege to the premises which were only defended by the landlord and barman, plus a waterworks engineer.

The rampaging crowd were out for blood and attacked the pub with anything they could lay hold of. The demon drink had thrust murder into their hearts. It was only after two drunken navvies were shot down by the defenders that the infuriated pack finally dispersed.

When twenty policemen and a doctor eventually arrived, all that remained was the mindless devastation left for the locals to clear up. As you walk south through the village, all is at peace with no reminders of the battle that took place here all those years ago.

Inside the churchyard by the door stands a huge stone block converted into a sundial. This was the seat which the Reverend Robert Walker used to sit upon whilst clipping his sheep at Gaitskell Farm around the middle of the 18th century. Known as 'Wonderful Walker' because of good works bestowed upon his human flock, the good cleric was no slouch when it came to shearing the four-legged variety.

Not only that, he also spun and wove his own cloth and toted raw wool on his back for sale at Broughton market seven miles away. Not especially a Herculean task in the days when walking was the only means of transport for the majority. But when you consider that he was also a teacher, will-writer, doctor, honey-maker, tanner and brewer in addition to raising eight children, Robert Walker must indeed have been a remarkable character, and one who was revered throughout the locality.

He always claimed that thrift and hard work were the essential elements for a long and fruitful life. He was certainly not wrong in this assumption. After serving as the resident incumbent for sixty-seven years, 'Wonderful Walker' finally passed on in 1802 at the grand age of ninety three.

The Walk

After pausing for a moment's reflection at his grave, walk through the village past the New Field Inn until you reach the first house on the left. Opposite is the start of a path which leads down to cross Tarn Beck by way of a stone footbridge.

Bear left along the wooded bank of the beck through carpets of bluebells (only if you arrive in spring) until it merges with the River

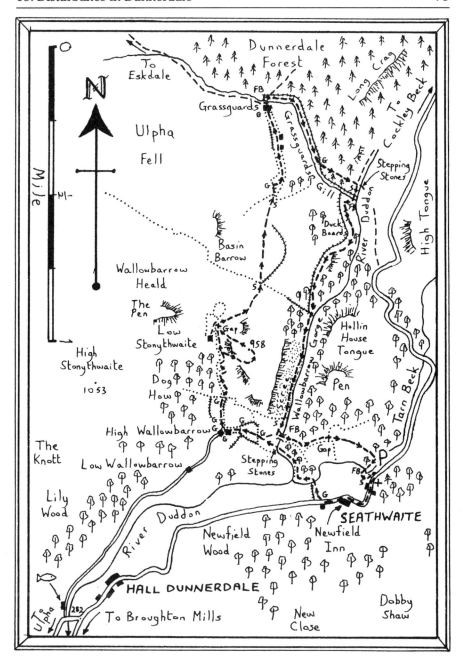

Duddon. Continue upstream through the woods to its outflow from Wallowbarrow Gorge where a set of stepping stones is provided for crossing the river. Apart from the initial hesitancy caused by a less than adequate boulder, onward progress is easily and safely assured. Those who doubt their ability to remain dry-footed should make use of the footbridge located a further 200 metres upstream.

On the far side, the path soon reaches the edge of the woodland before crossing a field to High Wallowbarrow. Enter the farmyard through a pair of gates then head right through another up an enclosed track that becomes a stony climb into the constricted tributary vale of Rake Beck. The rough path zigzags uphill through the woodland and then fords the chattering stream as the dense foliage is left behind.

Ahead, the imposing bastion of Wallowbarrow Crag presents an impregnable frontage that might well deter all but the hardiest rock hound. Not so. For those intrepid adventurers with liquid cement in their veins, an exhilarating yet quite easy scramble enables the summit ramparts to be breached.

Watch for a thin trod slanting right up to the base of the precipice. It then bears right avoiding the crag face to mount a series of heathery rock steps. There are no paths on the summit which comprises a rocky bluff that would certainly benefit from a cairn. If each new arrival were to carry a stone up from below, a fitting adornment would soon be constructed. From this lofty perch, enjoy the undulating scenery along the entire stretch of the valley twisting and turning unexpectedly between a succession of scabrous knolls.

To the north, the periphery of Dunnerdale Forest marks a change in the vegetation pattern from indigenous broadleaf to the controlled growth of conifers by the Forestry Commission. Planting began in 1934 and has always taken due heed of aesthetic connotations. Norway and Sitka Spruce interspersed with larch and selected hardwoods have tended to enhance the amenity value. Such development is to be heartily endorsed.

Looking down to the west at the head of Rake Beck, the renovated farmhouse of Low Stonythwaite affords what must rank as the most isolated private dwelling in Lakeland. Unless, of course, you know different. Vehicular access is restricted by an exceedingly rough track across open moorland and through dense forest. What a perfect locale to cast off the cares and tribulations of the rat race.

A simple stroll down the gently shelving western slopes of Wallowbarrow will bring you back to the main track close to a gap in the accompanying wall. Associates of a more easy-going disposition will be chafing at the bit to be on their way having already consumed their lunch, and yours too probably.

At this point, the track veers away from Low Stonythwaite across open moorland heading north towards Grassguards and the forest edge. As the farm is approached along an enclosed corridor, pay heed to the cluster of ruins now little more than overgrown field walls. On the right is presented a poser that I am still attempting to work out. How did that caravan manage to site itself in such a small enclosure? Answers on a postcard only, please!

At Grassguards, turn left upstream for fifty metres to cross the cascading beck on a footbridge. Return along the far bank crossing the main track near the ford. Continue down a narrow path between a fence and Grassguards Gill. Beyond the fence gate, the path enters the gloomy interior of maturing conifers to descend a rough outcropping as it slants away from the tumbling gill.

The final gradient is more acute as the valley bottom is neared amid the sombre and oppressive silence that always seems to accompany any walk through dense conifer plantings. To reach the far shore of the Duddon, assistance is delivered by a set of worn stepping stones. A safe crossing is achieved by the provision of a steel cable strung across the burbling current. Keeping the wet stuff at bay, however, is something else again. Try it at your peril.

Our route lies to the right crossing Grassguards Gill by means of a footbridge where it feeds into the river. Lean away from the river following a fence to avoid the marshy bottom-land making use of a pair of duckboards. Soon after, the path climbs above the river and the tree line.

As the gorge of Wallowbarrow is neared, the path again returns to the river bank where a fence stile is crossed. On either side, the glowering overhang of fractured crags remains hidden by the dominant sheath of hazel and birch woodland.

Continuing south down the gorge, the path crosses the lower limits of a belt of heavy scree. Here, the full might of the Wallowbarrow Crag is revealed. Huge blocks weighing several tons have come to rest in the river bed, the apocalyptic result of weathering and frost action on the splintered rock tableau above.

Just beyond a wall stile, cross to the far side of the river using a well-constructed footbridge, gated at either end. Follow a wall out of the woods below the knobbly outlier of Pen to cross the lowland pastures into the tree girt edge of Tarn Beck. Bear right over a small footbridge circling left to emerge onto the valley road at our starting point.

Not since that fateful day back in 1904 has the peaceful serenity of this lovely dale been again so violently shattered and hopefully it never will be. 'Wonderful Walker' can rest in peace in the full knowledge that the example he set of "temperance, industry and integrity" has become a by-word that few would choose to deny.

14. On Stony Ground

Mysteries:	Priapus Stone, GR 267741. Druids' Circle, GR 293739. Quaker Sepulchre, GR 286739
Distance:	5½ miles
Total height climbed:	460 feet/140 metres
Nearest centre:	Great Urswick
Start & finish:	A paved parking area is available next to the church of St Michael in Great Urswick.
Maps:	Ordnance Survey 1:25000. Pathfinder 635, Barrow-in-Furness (North) sheet.

Nestling within a secluded limestone basin, Urswick Tarn, the largest natural tarn in the area, provides an ideal setting from which to explore the artefacts characteristic of Low Furness. Clustered around the reed-fringed pool lies the village of Great Urswick with its grey stoned cottages. Recent housing tacked onto the south-west corner of the village does naught to detract from the placid serenity of this hoary settlement playing host to commuters who work in local towns.

Many of the buildings date back to the 17th century, the oldest being the General Burgoyne, one of two pubs serving this tiny village. Pronounced 'Ossick', its origins can be traced back to the Norman Conquest although much of the area enjoys a far greater antiquity. A brief scan of the Ordnance Survey map will reveal much evidence of settlement dating back to pre-history, all of which enhances that perception of latent mystery emanating from the Urswick hollow.

On a summer's day with sunlight glinting off the calm waters of the tarn where fishermen idly cast their lines, little of this inherent mysticism is felt. Yet an obscure legend suggests that the Great Urswick of today is but of recent construct having risen up from the bones of a doomed predecessor.

During a period of severe draught, complaints from local women urged the priest of St Michael's to "pray for water instead of wasting time on masses". This he endeavoured to do with the result that heavy rains came turning the water supply a turgid brown. Now the women grumbled that their cattle refused to drink the tainted water. So once again, the harassed cleric prayed for change. But on this occasion, a deluge filled the hollow destroying the entire village, except that is for the priest and his church. A clear message to those who were scathing of God's messenger and so paid the ultimate price.

Heavily fortified against marauding hoards, the squat church tower is built in a similar style to the pele towers of Lakeland. Likewise, it gave protection from at least two incursions in the 14th century under the leadership of Robert the Bruce. Known to be of Norman origin, the present structure is founded upon an even earlier Saxon church. Indeed, it is well known that Urswick existed before the monks of Furness Abbey spread their ecclesiastical and agrarian influence across the district.

Before setting out on this retrospective walk, take a stroll along the road past the church towards Little Urswick for about 200 metres. Watch out for a huge block of eroded limestone set into the base of the stone wall on your right.

This is the *Priapus Stone*. An ancient phallic symbol of fertility, it stood upright in the adjoining field until the 1920s. From early times until 1810, it was the village custom to decorate the stone on Midsummer's Day in the hope that fruitful procreation would result. Priapus hails from the Era of Greek mythology and was always represented as a man of repellent ugliness. Perhaps this is why the villagers decided he was rather an inappropriate emissary of fertility.

The Walk

Returning to the church car park, take the narrow signposted path along the left side of the churchyard. At the terminus of this short corridor, the way is blocked by an abundance of rubble fronting a broken gate. Veer right through a stile into the church yard then immediately left through another into the field beyond the obstruction.

Cross the flat grassy sward alongside a fence, then over a footbridge crossing the stream from Urswick Tarn. Although a balmy day in August when I beheld the mirrored surface, winters can be ferocious in Low Furness. Merrymaking and nimble-footed dancing were common practice in the 18th century when the tarn froze solid. An especially hard year was 1763 when a bull was roasted on the ice and racing took place.

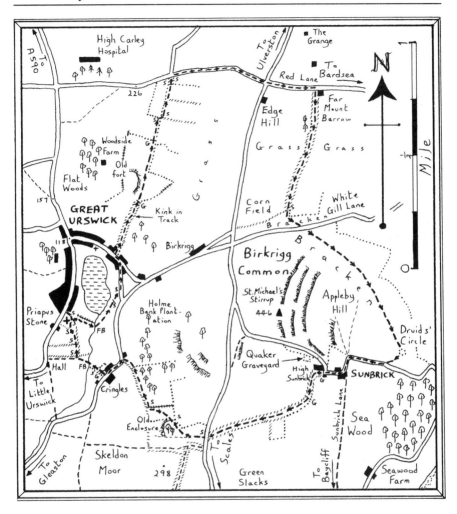

Bear half left heading north-east around the southern fringe of the tarn. Make sure to use the isolated kissing gate in the middle of the field, now lonely and forlorn since the hedge departed. Continue ahead to join a back lane through a stile where you should turn north up to the village road which circles the tarn.

Turn left back towards the village centre but leave this road after 100 metres to strike uphill on a hedged track. A major right-of-way leaving the Urswick basin, it points unerringly to the ancient hill fort on top of Skeldon Heads. A gate at the end of the enclosed section leads onto open grass where the ring of exposed limestone indicates the outer ramparts of the citadel.

Although no evidence can be seen of past settlement, numerous discoveries of tools and iron age implements prove that this flat crown was most definitely a Brigantean stronghold. There could be no more strategic site hereabouts sufficient to counter the attention of unwelcome intruders.

Return to the path and continue north on the left of a wall there to pass through a gate. Keep on to the next cross wall where two stiles in the off-set wall ensure that the correct route is taken on the opposite side of the continuing wall. A short walled passage at the end brings us to the east-west Bardsea road.

Head right for three-quarters of a mile and over a cross-roads until Far Mount Barrow is reached. Take the hedged path just before the building which heads south for another three-quarters of a mile. At the far end, cross a stile and fork left up a broad grass avenue scything through the bracken to reach the fell road.

On the far side, a broad expanse of rising open moorland cloaked in dense bracken is split by parallel chains of limestone scarring. Birkrigg Common is criss-crossed by a network of paths latticing the bracken sheath. Gently graded, the paths are a delight to follow as you maintain a general south-easterly course around the north shoulder of Appleby Hill.

Birkrigg is well known as a fine viewpoint across the Leven estuary which can be savoured on the stroll down the seaward slope towards the *Druids' Circle*. This most notable antiquity of Bronze Age settlement in Low Furness is easily missed, surrounded as it is by waist high bracken in summer. The ring of limestone boulders dating from 2100 BC rest amid a sheep-nibbled turf clearing. Beneath, the foundations of the mystic circle, although unseen, are known to have been carefully paved using stones hauled up from the Bardsea shoreline.

Stone circles abound throughout Lakeland, the largest being at Castlerigg near Keswick. Yet little is known of their purpose beyond functions associated with religious ceremonies and burials. Solar observatories, seasonal calendars and temples to the gods have also been suggested, all of which add to the air of mystery surrounding them.

Maybe the Druid cult did perform bizarre rituals at a time when fire,

The Druids' Circle

earth and water formed the very essence of their being. But who knows what strange beliefs and superstitions are ultimately based on truth? Nonetheless, let your imagination run riot, a feat of consummate ease if a sea mist rolls up from the shore to envelop this primeval site in its fetid embrace.

Join the open fell road heading uphill to the hamlet of Sunbrick which dates back to the middle ages. Meaning *swine-break*, this was an open glade where pigs once grubbed for acorns encompassed within a much more extensive covering of trees. Only the small acreage of Sea Wood now remains of the vast forest that disappeared following its clearance for agricultural usage.

After passing the initial buildings, turn right along the road as it climbs onto the scars of Birkrigg Common. Follow the field wall on your left up to a stone entrance porch which provides access to a square enclosure carpeted in grass and thistles.

This sheltered compound marks the site of the Society of Friends Sunbrick Burial Ground whose custom was to inter deceased members of their sect in unmarked graves. In all, 227 brethren were buried here between 1654 and 1767, the most eminent being the wife of George Fox, the movement's founder. Margaret Fox died at Swarthmoor Hall in 1702 at the age of 87 years.

A moment of silent reflection on the brevity of life's fickle passing should encourage us all to think hard on our chosen course. Certainly the wisest decision you have made of late was the purchase of this august volume illustrating a myriad of curious happenings in South Cumbria. Before leaving, take heed of the large slab abutting the north wall which pays tribute to the resident internees. Barely discernible, it remains the only visible memorial permitted by Quaker doctrine.

Return to High Sunbrick and turn right past the farmhouse through a tubular gate. Farmed by the Parker family for over 50 years, the present landlord is more than willing to impart local knowledge to passing ramblers. The hedged lane bears sharp left before leaning to the right as it slants down to the Scales road.

Cross the road and over a wall stile aiming half right across the field and keeping right of an old tree-girt enclosure of pristine conception. Merging with the wall on your right for 100 metres, the faint trod then bears left around the grassy shoulder north of the enclosure site dropping down to the field corner.

Beyond the fence stile, keep the hedge on your left through the open sconce of woodland scattered across this steep flank of Holme Bank Plantation. A further stile will deposit you on the back lane near a newly built residence. (At the time of writing, the right-of-way passed through the building site and the footpath sign had been snapped off).

Turn left down the lane, noting that a once substantial pool abutting Holme Bank has now dried up. Whether this is a sign of changing climatic patterns, or merely because of an unusually dry summer, remains to be seen. Bear right after the farm through a gate and then over a wall stile to cross Urswick Beck by way of a short footbridge.

Continue ahead across the corner of the next field to locate a hidden stile in the thorny hedge. Head north with a field hedge on your right to pass through another stile. Then break left away from the hedge to enter the hallowed grounds of St Michael's churchyard. Unfortunately, the interior is now barred to casual visitors following the erection of a locked iron gate across the main entrance. Seek out the verger should your curiosity as to the secrets within this noble edifice be unquenchable.

The path passes behind the church to emerge at the starting point. No other walk in this series emits such an overwhelming aura of primordial history, the past resonating with every step around this age old domain. Mysteries that are tangible if somewhat defused by the nebulous haze of antiquity assume a more immediate priority.

15. Bewitching Tebay

Mysteries:	Mary Baines, GR 617051. The Watcher, GR 645055
Distance:	6 miles
Total height climbed:	450 feet/137 metres
Nearest centre:	Tebay
Start & finish:	Driving north out of Old Tebay towards Orton on the B6260, a large parking area is available at the edge of the village on the left.
Maps:	Ordnance Survey 1:25000, Pathfinder 607, Tebay and Kirkby Stephen sheet.

First to recognise the strategic significance of a site at the entrance to the Lune Gorge was the Roman leader Agricola. It was he who first established a fort at Low Borrowbridge. Known as Alauna, it protected this important trade route through the northern fell country in addition to controlling rapacious insurgents from across the Border. A later *motte and bailey* fort located at Castle Howe was further testament to the importance of the site.

It was not until the 19th century that Tebay found itself to be ideally situated as a focus for transport links where road, rail and river converged at the mouth of the gorge. Prospering as an influential railway junction, the village grew to prominence extending in linear fashion down the current A685 south of the roundabout.

Following the closure of the north-eastern branch line under the Beeching cuts of 1962, the final denouement arrived six years later. Since the closure of the station, the only outward sign of the village's link with the railway age is the aptly named Junction Hotel. Trains regularly whistle past, disregarding the rather sad cluster of cottages that once housed the railway workers.

Separated by the A685 which follows the course of the eastern branch line, Old Tebay was originally a small farming community named after an elusive landowner called *Tibba*. One of the cottages was home to an old woman with an unpopular reputation for causing all manner of odious happenings in the village.

If the milk turned sour in the churn, a calf died at birth, geese attacked their herdsman, or a horse bolted, then Mary Baines was to blame. Many claimed she was a witch with unholy powers. Indeed, one story is told of Ned Nissen who ran the Cross Keys Inn and owned a brutish hound which killed poor Mary's black cat. Full of remorse, the landlord instructed his servant to give the animal a decent burial in her garden.

Not being as benevolent to the alleged witch as his master, the fellow ignored the prayer she had given him to say over the cat's grave. With total disregard for Mary's feelings, he grabbed the animal by a leg and uttered this importune ditty

Ashes to ashes, dust to dust,
Here's a hole and in tha must.

The angry woman threw a curse on the uncivil braggart as he swaggered off back to the Inn. Soon after while attending to his crops in a field nearby, the plough jumped up and the handle struck his head causing instant blindness. Some believed it to be the work of Mary Baines although nothing was done about it.

In those distant times when superstition was rife, many such women accused of witchcraft were harassed and persecuted. Mary Baines was one of the lucky ones dying peacefully in her bed in 1811 at the age of 80 years. One of her last known predictions was that "carriages without horses shall run across Loups Fell." Now universally known as Shap, this prophecy came to fruition in the 1840s when the Lancaster-Carlisle Railway was opened.

As recently as 1983, a photograph of a steam train chugging past the old junction revealed the figure of a mysterious woman wearing a cloak. Claiming she had not been present when the picture was taken, the photographer was convinced that here was Mary Baines returned to the scene of her last oracle.

The Walk

To begin this walk, take the rough lane that leads down to the banks of the River Lune. Pass through a gate followed immediately by another on the right to join an overgrown pathway alongside the river. This is clearly not often used. A disintegrating weir indicates an early attempt to control the river's flow for the benefit of local farmers.

As I approached Tebay Bridge, a skein of geese shot from beneath the arched mouth in tight formation and flew down towards the motorway.

With the panache of an attacking force of harriers, they skimmed the rippling surface with the clear intention of blasting this elongated interloper that had invaded their territory. Never previously have I witnessed such a splendid display of bravado from a feathered squadron of *top guns*.

Join the B6260 and cross the Lune leaving the road at the far side of the bridge through a stile. The path accompanies a thin tributary before slanting left across a field. Beyond a wall stile, the path merges with a major access track serving Coatflatt Hall. After crossing Chapel Beck, bear right towards the hall but fork left through a gate behind the group of buildings that comprise this old farming settlement.

Take a walk along the walled lane which angles sharp left at the end of the cottages pointing the way up a rising grass bank. Keeping to the right of a wall, we pass through a corner gap and diagonally across the next field. Another gap, followed immediately by a gate, brings us along the left side of a wall which is accompanied to a sheep pen with the name of Far Garth. Across the valley, the northern slopes of the Howgills rise up in nonchalant ease like a herd of carousing hippos.

Here the right-of-way again changes to the far side of the wall which is then followed down the easy grass slope to valley level. Go through a gate and across the next field to reach the B6261 just south of Raigill Hall. Over Rais Beck, yellow arrow markers act as a guide through the array of farm buildings. Beyond the last gate, our route rises left, above and behind the hall, where a wall stile should be located.

Follow the wall eastwards to another stile thereafter continuing across open grass slopes above the river. Three more stiles are to be negotiated at the upper limit of the valley tree-line before entering more extensive woodland. The path then begins to descend as the final wall is crossed. Drop down to Rayne Bridge gained up a short wooden stairway allowing access to the road through a gap stile.

Linger awhile at this special place which stimulated a local school teacher to effuse in eloquent tribute over the rich and varied wildlife observed from the bridge. Times innumerable during the early years of this century, Thomas Bowness-Wright walked the quarter mile from his cottage in Rayne to enjoy the peace and tranquillity of the rustic scene. His intimate recollections were minutely detailed with the eye of a born naturalist in letters that he sent to friends.

Many of these literary chronicles were collected and arranged into a book entitled *The Watcher by the Bridge*. Published after his death in

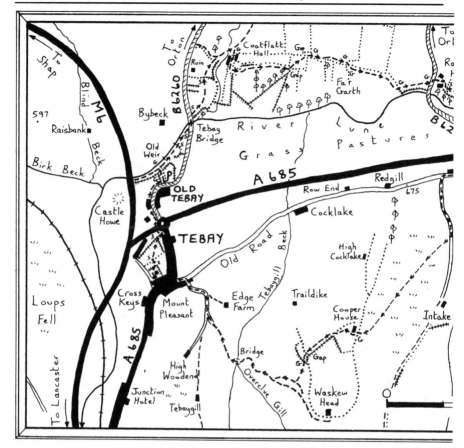

1936, this classic tome captures the very essence of life on the river bank. In vivid manner, it outlines the shrouded antics of creatures that only a dedicated observer could ever hope to describe. Otters were his particular favourites and many were the hours that Bowness-Wright spent in silent contemplation of their enthralling capers.

If you have enjoyed tarrying awhile in contemplation of this serene locale "until the blue haze fills the head of the gorge and an unearthly solemnity seems to fold you to itself", then *The Watcher* is most definitely a book to be eagerly sought.

At some point, it will be necessary to drag yourself away from this picturesque idyll and head west towards the main road. After 100 metres, a dilapidated barn on the left is passed bearing the bold legend

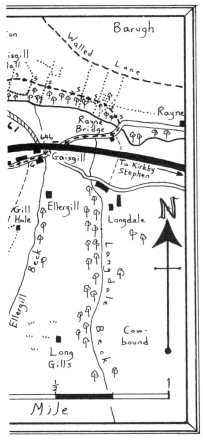

"This building has been entered for the Guildway National Quality Award, 1975". Does the owner possess an irreverent sense of humour, or is he just an eternal optimist? A classic aberration if ever there was one.

Cross the A685 to reach the tiny hamlet of Gaisgill remembering that you are now accompanying the original road to Kirkby Stephen before the conversion of the old rail line. Dominated by a petrol station, it does have a Wesleyan Chapel of some distinction built in 1841.

Continue along the road towards Tebay noting the right-of-way on the left through a gate. Upon attempting to make use of this, I was promptly informed by the householder opposite that this was private land with no public access. Not wishing to dispute this claim having a twelve-year-old map in my possession, I carried on to use the metalled farm road serving Gill Hole and Intake.

Confirmation on the latest OS sheet revealed that there is indeed a direct right-of-way across the fields to Gill Hole. The local Ramblers' Association have been informed of this anomaly and as of writing (August, 1996), are investigating whether the route still exists.

Whichever route you choose, fork right off the paved highway along a distinct fell track. Too soon, when this comforting guide dissolves into the marshy tract of tough upland grass, maintain a south-westerly bearing. Ahead, the ruin of Cooper House provides a landmark to aim for. Once there, go through the gate adjoining the bones of this once thriving hill farm. Like many such abandoned settlements hereabouts, the spirits of long departed residents flit amongst the skeletal remains in silent tribute to a declining lifestyle.

Beyond Cooper House, follow a broken wall across rough pasture to the corner of a new fence. Accompany the fence on your left across a broken wall and round to a gate. Cross an open grass sward to join the track serving another old settlement at Waskew Head. Turn right here and descend the tortuous trail to cross Tebaygill Beck by a substantial stone bridge.

Follow this major track which becomes metalled as Edge Farm is approached on your right. Below lies New Tebay, soon reached by sticking with this fell access road. It is worth recalling on the descent that the village witnessed a violent struggle in 1885. Two notorious villains were arrested here following a particularly heinous robbery committed in Carlisle, involving the murder of a pursuing constable. A third collaborator managed to escape but was later arrested in Lancaster.

Detraining at Tebay, the gang attempted to pervert the course of justice by secreting the stolen jewellery in the River Lune. Hoping to return and claim the swag at some future date, their plans were thwarted by the local constabulary who returned them to Carlisle for trial. Found guilty, the infamous trio was hanged on a specially erected gallows. The first execution at Carlisle jail for ten years attracted morbid onlookers from all over the country and was carried out by a professional hangman at 8am on the 8th of February, 1886. Their bodies were interred within the boundaries of the jail until 1928 when the bones were exhumed and re-buried in the city graveyard, the exact location of which remains a mystery. The lost jewels were, however, safely recovered from the river bed after the felons confessed under the misapprehension that mercy would be shown.

Today, the village is a quiet and unobtrusive place. Turn left down the main street towards the celebrated Cross Keys brought to public attention through the cabalistic activities of Mary Baines and her cat. Bear right down Church Street taking the first right along a back passage.

The right-of-way passes left of the new doctor's surgery to mount a fence stile at the back. Cross the next field aiming for a wall stile near a newly fenced planting of young trees. Thereafter, descend the grass slope to the far right corner where a fence stile allows free passage across a private garden to reach the main road close to the roundabout.

On the far side is the B6260, along which you stroll through the village of Old Tebay and back to the car. Speculation as to which of the cottages housed Mary Baines should be tempered with an awareness of the fear and alarm such old women engendered in those far off days. In fact, when modernisation of these old houses was undertaken, pots of bent pins used to counter the influence of witchcraft are known to have been unearthed.

16. Girt Will O' the Tarns

Mysteries:	The Giant's Grave, GR 314996; Caldron Dub, GR 304981
Distance:	5½ miles
Total height climbed:	530 feet/162 metres
Nearest centre:	Coniston
Start & finish:	Turn right up the Hodge Close lane just beyond High Yewdale Farm and park on the left close to Shepherd's Bridge.
Maps:	Ordnance Survey English Lakes, 1:25000, south-west area sheet.

North of Coniston, Yewdale Beck squeezes out of its constricting flue between defiant turrets of naked rock. Clearly relieved at having escaped the restraint imposed by its rugged origins, the watercourse breaths more freely as it wanders idly down the sylvan dale to feed into Coniston Water.

This mellow glen has for centuries pursued its pastoral traditions undeterred by the constant increase in traffic along the main artery between Ambleside and Coniston. Who, therefore, could possibly surmise that such a placid scene has witnessed murder and mayhem on a grand scale. Yet such is the tale of *Girt Will 'o the Tarns*.

Reckoned to be over nine feet (three metres) in height, the 'Giant of Yewdale' arrived from Troutbeck about the middle of the 18th century. Initially feared because of his huge stature, Will's hard work and amiable disposition soon endeared him to the local populace.

Lord of the Manor was Sir William Fleming who lived at Coniston Hall with his beautiful daughter who had an equally comely maid named Barbara. It was she to whom Girt Will became enamoured. One day whilst strolling on the banks of the lake, the two ladies were accosted by the giant who attempted to ingratiate himself with the maid.

His advances spurned, Will became irate and grabbed Barbara making off with her into the surrounding woodland. Lady Eva immediately dashed back to the Hall for assistance. Upon learning of his betrothed's predicament, Dick Hawksley, a young falconer in the employ of Sir William, gathered a posse and set off in hot pursuit of the rascally giant.

They soon overtook him at Caldron Dub whereupon the distraught falconer pleaded for Barbara'a release. Eaten up by lust and thwarted ambition, Will threw the poor girl into the swirling waters of the Dub now swollen by a recent downpour. The girl was immediately swept downstream. Seeing the life of his loved one in mortal danger, Hawksley dived in to save her, but the raging torrent was too fierce and both were dragged under.

Meanwhile, the giant had scuttled off in the direction of Holme Fell to make good his escape. Realising the young lovers were doomed, the others resumed their hunt for the villain who had perpetrated such a dastardly crime.

Approaching the narrowing head of Yewdale, Girt Will stood his ground and fought off his attackers with spirited defiance. But they were too many, and soon the 'Giant of Yewdale' fell beneath a welter of swords and arrows, his bleeding torso a testament to the remorseless pangs of unrequited passion.

The reputed grave of Girt Will in Yewdale

The Walk

Buried at the spot where he died, a twelve foot mound can be seen right of the path as you head south from the main road close to High Yewdale Farm. This path, initially on the left of a fenced and slabbed field boundary, slants half right beyond a stile to cross the next field. Through the next gate, keep straight ahead to mount a stile and so accompany a fence on your left to Low Yewdale.

At the far side of the farm buildings, bear right along the access road to reach the main road. Cross straight over and through a stile to enter the fringe of woodland skirting the road. Turn left towards Coniston soon crossing a wall stile and bearing right away from the road across open ground. Over another stile and you re-enter Whins Wood to follow a clear trail below the towering ramparts above.

A profuse array of boulders litters the floor of the wood all smeared with a verdant coating of Yewdale moss. Cross the tumbling waters of White Beck on a footbridge. Thereafter, the path continues south-west eventually veering towards the highway opposite a sawmill.

Walk down the road for 200 metres crossing to the far side at a distinct kink. Here then is the infamous Caldron Dub (pronounced locally as *kernel*) where murder most foul was committed. Following the tragic episode, the two bodies were swept downstream clutched in each other's arms. They were not discovered until the following week on the shores of Coniston still clasped in a prophetic embrace.

It will emerge as no surprise to learn that the Dub is haunted. The ghostly apparition of Girt Will has frequently been seen flitting between the stands of oak and birch, perhaps trying to atone for his heinous iniquity. When the beck is in spate, the screams of a drowning woman are said to have been heard to rent the air in mortifying paroxysms.

Think well on the woeful circumstances that led to this tragedy in Yewdale as you stroll down past Caldron Dub. Take the left turn along the Hawkshead road until you reach Shepherd Bridge on the left. Cross the beck and a small stile at its far side to head back upstream. After passing through a fence stile, aim to the right of a wall across an open field keeping right of this up to an old ruin (fenced off and under repair at the time of writing).

Go through a stile to skirt the ruin and then climb an easy bank up to a gate. The main trail, here part of the *Cumbria Way*, continues ahead. Our route forks right along a re-routed way uphill towards the wooded

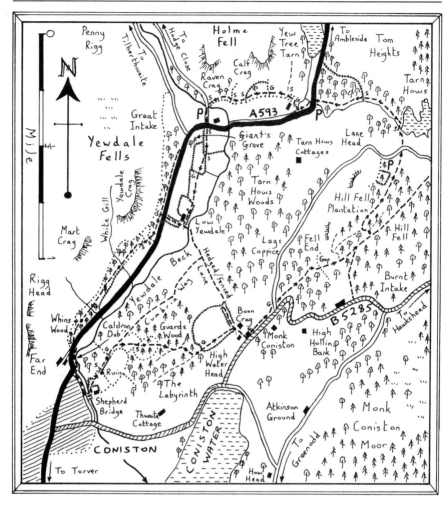

knoll of High Guards. Aim midway along the wall and cross a stile to the wooded enclave.

Pass over the apex through a wall gap and down the far side to merge with a rutted forest track. After 100 metres, fork right down between conifers to meet the old right-of-way which has now been abandoned. The edge of the wood is soon reached thereafter. Beyond the gate, follow a fence to a major cross-valley route.

Bear right through the cluster of buildings that make up Boon Crag Farm, now a base for the National Park Ranger Service. Turn left up the

B5285 secondary road joining the roadside path after Boon Crag cottage. Emerging onto the Tarn Hows road after a quarter of a mile, cross over into thick woodland.

A broad path climbs the left bank of a stream. Take note of a series of unusual dams higher up like a flight of canal locks. What is their purpose?

Stick with this clear trail ignoring all red herrings to right and left until the second signpost is reached. Here take the path to the left that swings left in a wide loop before continuing north up to the car park at Tarn Hows. This dense woodland is home to wild deer: shy creatures that are occasionally seen.

Cross the road and make your way onto the prominent knoll rising on the far side. On a crisp autumn day, with leaves tinged every shade of rustic hue, the views are second to none. A light flurry of snow dusting the Langdale Pikes will set them off in syncopated harmony against the azure curtain behind.

All who come to the Lake District have Tarn Hows on their itinerary, a fact likely to ensure a constant stream of visitors throughout the year. Yet how many realise that the name refers to the hill on which you are now standing rather than the waters below.

Once a series of loose tarns within a marshy basin, the water level was raised in the last century by a dam erected at the south-west corner. The resultant stretch ensconced between a select planting of extraneous trees has become one of the most renowned beauty spots in the country, epitomising as it does the softer side of Lakeland.

Most people simply park up and walk round the tarn. But how well I remember taking a short cut directly across to the far side. Not in a boat, nor did I hitch a ride with a passing trout. In December of 1961, the tarn froze over much to the delight of skaters who skimmed effortlessly across the glistening ice, a weak sun glinting off their shiny blades.

Wordsworth also experienced the joy of winter sports which he elucidated in *The Prelude* thus:

> "...*All shod with steel*
> *We hissed along the polished ice in games*
> *Confederate, imitative of the chase.*"

Take a stroll down to the dam, passing through a stile and turning left down a narrow path. Follow the right bank of Tom Gill with its impressive cataracts bounding off the boulder strewn ravine. John Ruskin of Brantwood it was who re-named the beck *Glen Mary*, and this has now become its generally accepted title. Beyond a fence stile, the path meanders down through the woods past trees like alien invaders sprouting from the solid rock.

At the bottom, rejoin the A593 and head left towards Coniston. After 200 metres, bear right adjacent to Yew Tree Farm and then through a gate. The walled track bends left up a shallow gradient behind the farmhouse to a stile.

The path then follows a wall to the left, first passing through a gate followed by three stiles to the Hodge Close access road. Turn left over Shepherd's Bridge and Yewdale Beck to arrive back at the car, and the end of a stimulating walk prompting much thought and reflection on the vagaries of the human persona.

17. Through the 'Eye' of Cartmel

Mysteries:	The Twin Streams, GR 379789. Hampsfield Hospice, GR 399794. The Beggar's Breeches
Distance:	4½ miles
Total height climbed:	650 feet/198 metres
Nearest centre:	Cartmel
Start & finish:	Suitable parking is available in Cartmel Village near the Priory and on the main street. Bank Holidays and Race Days should be avoided when traffic congestion is likely to be heavy.
Maps:	Ordnance Survey 1:25000, Pathfinder 636 Grange-over-Sands.

When approaching Cartmel from any direction, there is no doubting the dominant feature that grabs the attention. Soaring above all other structures in the valley, St Mary's Priory cannot fail to impress even the most incredulous visitor. Solid and unyielding, an irrepressible legacy of early Christian endeavour, the early prior and his brethren followed *The Rule of St Augustine*.

Known as *Black Canons* because of their dark cloaks, the order pursued an elaborate ritual of daily observances enclosed with in the grounds of the priory. Only on very special occasions were they allowed to vacate the premises.

One can only surmise that the ascent of Hampsfield Fell would have been of sufficient import to justify such a release from pious duty. After all, closer contact with *The Boss* was not to be taken lightly. In those far off days when the human psyche placed a literal meaning on many aspects associated with Heaven and Hell, such reasoning would likely have been soundly approved.

Arriving here in the 12th century, the first canons went on to lay the foundations for a new church on what was felt to be the most fitting site. Where else but on a local hill? During these initial excavations, one of the brethren received a sign from on high that this was not a worthy site at all for God's House.

The edict stated that the church must be erected between two streams flowing in opposite directions. Could such a site be found? A difficult task but one which the monks determined to pursue with alacrity. Full of vigorous intent, they dispersed throughout the region.

After many months, they eventually returned to Cartmel having failed in their assignment. It was only by chance that a vigilant fellow noticed the contrary flow of parallel streams actually existed in their very midst.

At last, permanent foundations could be laid. On a bed of peat with no solid base was perhaps a somewhat ill-judged emplacement for such a mammoth structure. Yet the monks trusted in the Word of God and stuck to their task, a decision which has proved its validity over the intervening centuries.

The off-set belfry was added in the early 15th century both for economic reasons and to limit the strain imposed on supporting pillars. Certainly an unusual addendum, but 'striking' nonetheless assuring the building of a stalwart individuality.

The Lakeland poet Norman Nicholson once attempted to write a poem about the priory but only managed the first line before giving up. It began *God's box of bricks* . . . and this summed up his feelings that the church was "a huge child's castle of cubes".

Little new development has occurred to mar the rustic peace emanating from Cartmel whose narrow streets and passageways are a joy to explore. Set forth on this walk by first visiting the priory where regular services are preceded by a strident peal of bells.

Inside, one particular idiosyncrasy is to be found at the north-east corner of the nave. On a wooden shelf attached to a pillar, bread is left for distribution "to the most indigent housekeepers of this parish every Sunday for ever". Such was the bequest of Rowland Briggs, who died on 27th November 1703, with an added payment of 25 pence per year to the sexton and his successors "...to be paid every Christmas Day provided they keep his grave unbroken up".

Two small loaves stood upon the shelf on the Sunday I visited, and freshly baked too judging by the wholesome aroma being given off. Such undertakings were once pursued by philanthropic citizens conscious that many rural dwellers teetered on the brink of starvation. Today, they remain a quaint tradition acting as a poignant reminder of our own good fortune.

The Walk

Exit through the north door to reach the back lane. Turn right over the River Eea (pronounced 'eye') noting the southerly flow. A short distance further and we cross its narrow tributary heading north. At the main road, turn left for 50 metres before crossing to the opposite side and mounting some stone steps. A short passage signposted to Hampsfell Hospice and gated at the far end leads onto a large field.

Follow its right side along a hedge to Pit Farm where a low stile is crossed. Bear left then right to continue up a gently sloping field with a fence on the left. At the top and beyond a gate, accompany a wall on your left to pass through a gate in the final in-take boundary which is hedged.

After passing through the iron barred gate, the ground becomes much steeper as valley pasture is replaced by open fell country. Stunted hawthorn poke above the bracken, deformed and bent into grotesque positions like old men struggling uphill against the prevailing westerlies. A clear path points the way onto the grassy saddle of Hampsfield Fell.

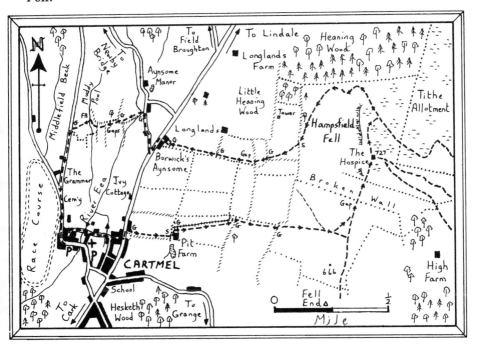

Initially veering to the right, it then heads left as the gradient eases to merge with the principal path along the crest of the broad ridge. Beyond the broken wall, aim for a more solid structure ahead to cross a stile and so reach the Hospice. This square monument is defended by a low ring of limestone scarring.

Erected by Thomas Remington, an avid walker and vicar of Cartmel from 1835 to 1854, the Hospice makes an ideal dry shelter for lunch. Above the doorway etched in stone, a Greek inscription intimates the noble cleric's favoured time of day. Meaning *The Rosy Fingered Dawn*, scholars of the classics will appreciate the sentiment more than the fell residents who are barred from entry by an iron gate.

On a clear day, the consummate panorama is all encompassing and the pivotal indicator can be used to identify visible landmarks. Particular note should be taken of the low hill at the southern limit of the Eea Valley. This is Mount Bernard where the original canons elected to build their church. At some later stage, a chapel was built in commemoration but of this, no evidence remains.

Whilst inside the enclosure, stimulate the mind, and the chuckle muscles, by sampling the witty ode that was penned by the good Reverend. An ancestor who took possession of the land at some later date was less than complementary to fell wanderers accusing us of having "more muscle than brain". Prove him a bigoted poltroon by leaving the Hospice in the clean manner you found it.

To the north on the highest part of the fell, a first rate limestone pavement should be visited. Clint blocks interlaced with deep grikes demonstrate the unique topography characteristic of limestone country. On the day I passed this way, freezing winds surging across the barren terrain brought to mind a particularly strange occurrence that happened back in 1799.

A beggar was found on the fell suffering from exposure following a severe frost. Carried down to Cartmel, he was revived by liberal doses of tea laced with gin. Unfortunately, he failed to recover and died soon after. In his breeches were discovered 185 guineas supposedly acquired through begging. In addition, a bogus medical certificate with an accompanying gall stone intimated that this was his method of securing the sympathetic remuneration.

It had certainly worked. But as with all attempts to hoodwink the benevolence of others, the perpetrator gets his comeuppance eventually. As the beggar had no kin, the money was put to good use for the benefit of the local poor and is still known as the *Charity of the Beggar's Breeches*.

To avoid the necessity of a similar fate, put your money in a bank. Or better still, keep to the clear path on leaving the Hospice to continue north along the ridge. Skirting left below the main pavement, the path circles round to the right meeting up with a major cross fell trail linking the Eea Valley and Grange. After forking into this, maintain a northerly course towards the massed phalanx of conifers ahead.

The clear trail bends left before the wall boundary as it circles back on itself down the western flank on the approach to the in-take hedge. Cross a stile and then diagonally down the field to a gate at the far left corner. Thereafter, accompany the wall on your left down to Borwick's Aynsome. Beyond the gated yard, turn left along the valley road.

After 100 metres, make a sharp right for a further 300 metres until the *lonely* settlement of Aynsome Mill is reached on the right. Go left through a gate to cross the youthful River Eea on a slate footbridge. Keep a hedge on your left to reach the far corner of the field. Here we go through another gate and carry on alongside a wall abutting a small copse. Two hedged gaps later and you will arrive at Muddy Pool which is crossed by a handy footbridge. A short climb up the facing grass bank will bring you to the back lane gained through a gate in the far left corner.

Turn left back towards Cartmel heading due south past the celebrated racecourse and left at the end into the main street of the village. Although a village that receives many visitors, Cartmel is a well-ordered settlement if appearing to be cramped. The houses are there to be lived in rather than merely looked at. Today, both village and priory are complementary, each dependent on the other.

18. Skulduggery at Hawkshead

Mysteries:	The Colthouse Quakers, GR 359981; The Hanging Tree, GR 355981; The Drunken Duck, GR 351013
Distance:	5½ miles
Total height climbed:	550 feet/168 metres
Nearest centre:	Hawkshead
Start & finish:	Park on the narrow lane behind the hamlet of Colthouse opposite the Quaker Meeting House.
Maps:	Ordnance Survey 1:25000 English Lakes, south-east area sheet.

A Quaker settlement dating back from the 17th century, Colthouse has changed but little over the intervening years unlike its larger neighbour. Hawkshead on the other hand has become a *honey pot* attracting visitors from far and wide. One reason for Hawkshead's renown could be the attendance of a young William Wordsworth at the grammar school, and his having lodged with Ann Tyson and her husband in a cottage close by.

Evidence has since come to light indicating that most of his time in the locality was actually spent at the good lady's abode across the valley in Colthouse. Few people venture into this tiny enclave where the inscrutable mists of a turbulent past linger untainted.

In consequence, one can easily slip back into a period when the residents practised their faith under the constant threat of persecution. Once the Church of England had re-established itself following the succession of the monarchy, all non-conformist doctrines suffered greatly at the hands of those who had old scores to settle.

Today, worshippers still gather in the Quaker Meeting House just as they did when it was first built in 1688. Walk south down the lane between the buildings that make up Town End Farm. Although having surrendered to the benefits of 20th century progress, the old water pump still remains as a reminder of how difficult life must have been for rural communities in those far off days.

Just beyond the farm on the left is a gate opening into the old burial ground set up in 1658 and one of the first to be reserved solely for

Quakers. Wall seats of slate offer a peaceful haven from external traumas where the simple headstones testify to an austere interpretation of Christian values.

Early Quakers did not believe in any headstones at all, claiming that such ostentation supported '*a worldley vanytie*'. It is only from the late 18th century that the present small rounded grave markers began to appear. Set out in neat rows, only the name and date of demise are carved into the grey stone.

From this tranquil oasis, make your way westwards across the causeway (pronounced *causey*) built across a broad tract of marshy peat. The wet nature of the ground on either side of the hedged road is clearly evident. Immediately before crossing the bridge over Black Beck on the left stands an isolated tree. Lonely and forbidding, it marks the spot where the local gibbet was erected in the 17th century.

One unfortunate recipient of the gibbet's terminal embrace was a certain Thomas Lancaster who in 1672 was accused of poisoning his entire family with arsenic in their food. Tried at Lancaster assizes (not because of his name but that being the county seat of law), the hapless felon was strung up in chains, there to remain "*untill such tymes as hee rotted everye bone from other...*". Verily a grizzly end to what can only be regarded as a heinous crime in which seven people succumbed and several others became violently ill.

Quite clearly, the second half of the 17th century was a time of ferment when passions ran high in the Esthwaite Valley. Consider well the fate of Thomas Lancaster and the Colthouse Quakers as you continue on towards Hawkshead. The main road crosses Black Beck by way of a Victorian bridge. Once painted an eye-catching green, the current grey of the iron panelling conforms much more to National Park guidelines in blending with the local environment.

Another 100 metres will bring you to the southern limit of Hawkshead and a car park that is almost the size of the village proper. At the T-junction, turn right as far as the entrance to St Michael's churchyard. If you can spare the time, a brief saunter around the nooks and ginnels that comprise this ancient settlement is recommended.

Quaint, picturesque, old-world, charming are all clichés that have been applied in abundance to the village by romantics over the years. And rightly so – Hawkshead equates to all these platitudes and more. Such adulation has, unfortunately, resulted in the settlement acquiring a "Goldfish Bowl Syndrome" with coach loads of tourists arriving to gape at the chocolate box cottages and sample the local tea rooms.

Its original growth as a market town concentrated on the production of wool. Local Herdwicks supplied the wool for stockings that were in great demand throughout the district and beyond. But it was the monks of Furness Abbey who ensured the importance of the village as a wool gathering centre in the 13th century. This followed the establishment of a grange farm at what was later to become the Hawkshead Courthouse located next to Hall Bridge. The Manor of Hawkshead thereafter became the richest possession of Furness Abbey.

The Walk

As you enter the paved courtyard abutting the church, take note of the old grammar school on the left where young William spent much of his early years. Pass through the graveyard emerging at its far side into a narrow passage with the local characteristic slab wall on the right. At a fork in the path following a stile, bear left alongside a hedge through a series of stiles which will carry you on a clear path to the old farming commune of Roger Ground.

Along with several others in the area, the 'grounds' date back to the early 16th century when the Furness monks enclosed the common pastures. Usually coupled with the surname of the family that created the farm, the adjoining field patterns are amongst the oldest in the Lake District to have survived from Tudor times.

Keep right up the Grizedale road for 50 metres before slanting left down a narrow lane serving a cluster of modern bungalows. After passing the last one with the name of 'Springfield', make use of a foot-bridge to cross a pair of streams feeding into Esthwaite at their point of convergence. Through the gate, follow one of the streams towards Howe Farm. Two gates carry you around to the left of the farm buildings away from the yard to reach the access track and thence down to the valley road.

Head right for a quarter of a mile before swinging right along a broad track serving a group of dwellings ensconced within this sylvan glade. Keep left through a gate abutting Elder Ghyll that has assumed the name of the beck scuttling down through the wooded glen of Elder Coppice. Climb the steepening track up the valley side until it opens out at a higher level into a broad grassy swathe.

Ford a tributary of Elder Ghyll and follow a series of way markers uphill on a newly created path. After a wall stile, continue up the grassy trail to High Barn and so along its access track to join the Grizedale road close to Moor Top. To the west and south, the expansive blanket of

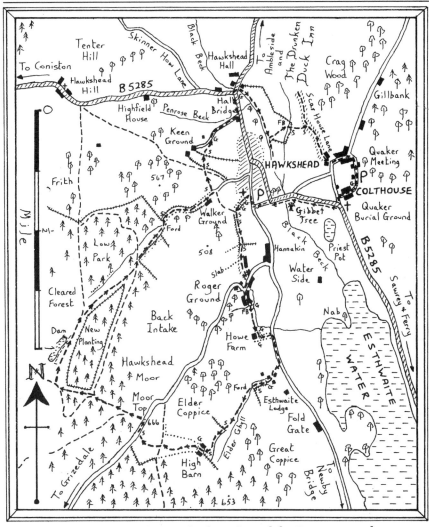

coniferous woodland that embodies Grizedale Forest stretches away into the distance. The ocean of dark green is criss-crossed by a myriad of nature trails and cycle tracks.

Acquired by the Forestry Commission in 1934 to encourage forestry, nature conservation and leisure, the Grizedale Valley took time out during the second world war in its role as host to German POWs. The camp is no longer there but a 'Theatre in the Forest' and visitor centre encourage a more appreciative clientele.

Stands of larch have been planted to encourage the continued breeding of indigenous red deer whose numbers have increased substantially in recent years. Young animals can, however cause harm to the trees and need culling at regular intervals.

Turn right along the road towards Hawkshead for 50 metres and then left along a forest trail. Beyond the car park, keep straight ahead ignoring a cycle track forking left. A quarter of a mile on and we arrive at a three-way junction. Take the rough, steeper arm again – keeping straight ahead through the welter of towering spruce and fir.

After merging with the main track, turn almost immediately right along a clear path that passes close to a sparkling gem of a tarn hidden away amidst this verdant mantle. Surely an ideal locale to linger awhile over a well-earned lunch.

Carry on along this trail noting the open tract on the left where mature trees have been felled. Such decimation is a frequent occurrence in forests where softwood timber is grown for commercial purposes. Like a 'no-man's-land' from the Great War, the cutting operation leaves behind a devastated landscape that no amount of care is capable of disguising.

Watch for a right fork down a side path alongside a youthful beck. A substantial fence on the right protects new conifers from the red deer which can cause irreversible damage to the young trees. After joining the lower cycle track, head left but take another right fork after 100 metres to continue down valley. Ford the stream close to the edge of the forest zone and soon after, enter an enclosed rough lane dropping down to Walker Ground.

Here, bear left through a stile across open parkland passing through a fence stile to descend the lush grass pasture adjacent to Keen Ground. The right-of-way merges with the farm access road connecting with the main road. Make a left turn along the B5286 as far as Hall Bridge and a T-junction.

Opposite the B5285, go through a gate and make your way along the side of Black Beck. According to the OS map, the right-of-way cuts directly across an open field but there is no path visible through the grass. In view of this appearing to be a growing crop, stick with the beck up to the fence barrier then bear left to join a distinct path. This crosses a minor stream by way of a foot-bridge and so through a hedge stile to join Scar House Lane at the far side of the valley.

Turn right along this old highway that still retains the characteristics associated with all roads serving the area in times past. Here is presented a perfect opportunity to immerse oneself in a Lake District that has largely disappeared and is now preserved only in faded snapshots. Entering the outer limits of Colthouse, head left past a number of cottages named after past residents and swing up the side road back to the Meeting House.

An apt finale to this revealing walk should be a visit to the Drunken Duck Inn, there to partake of some well-earned liquid refreshment whilst pondering over the origins of this quirky appellation. Formerly known as the Barngates Inn, this isolated hostelry stands at a crossroads one mile south of Skelwith Fold and is even mentioned by name on the OS map.

The story is told of a previous landlord who kept ducks behind the inn. On one particular occasion, a barrel of beer fell off the dray and smashed spilling the contents all over the yard. Unbeknown to the innkeeper, the ducks found the foaming brew to their taste and proceeded to sup the lot. On discovering them strewn about in a drunken stupor, he thought they were dead and instructed his wife to pluck the birds ready for the oven. It must have been a startling revelation for the poor woman when the ducks awoke, no doubt suffering from a king-sized hangover. Feeling sorry for the birds in their naked state and a mite guilty, she set to and knitted them each a woollen overcoat to wear until their feathers grew back.

The Drunken Duck Inn

19. Blawith Secrets

Mysteries:	The Silent Bell, GR 289833. The Giant's Grave, GR 256879
Distance:	6 miles
Total height climbed:	650 feet/200 metres
Nearest centre:	Blawith
Start & finish:	Park on the grass verge abutting the old section of road now by-passed at Blawith.
Maps:	Ordnance Survey 1:25000 Pathfinder Series 626 – Broughton-in-Furness and Newby Bridge.

Draining out of Coniston Water, the River Crake pursues an amiable course south towards the Kent estuary at Greenodd. Placid and largely undisturbed by the passage of visitors bound for the heartland of the District, there is little to indicate the industrial heritage of this once booming community.

In the early days of the Industrial Revolution, hazel, oak and birch coppice woodland that lined the Crake furnished the charcoal essential to a burgeoning iron industry. Spark Bridge, Penny Bridge and Nibthwaite flourished in the 18th century as a result of the increased trade generated. Small arms and cannon shot are known to have been manufactured at Nibthwaite for use in the crushing of the 1745 Scots Rebellion. Except for the old forge oven which still survives, however, all the scars of man's endeavour within the industrial arena have long since healed over.

Today the valley has reverted to its agrarian roots and remains undisturbed by the modern influx of tourists. Indeed, according to local opinion, the valley could well benefit from re-generation to stimulate both the social and community infrastructure.

Blawith in particular has suffered in this respect, a repercussion that led to the closure of its second church. Herein lies the outcome of a bizarre tale that began over 200 years ago. Pronounced 'Blaath' with a long 'a', the meaning stems from old Norse meaning the *dark woodland*. Now virtually devoid of forest cover on this side of the valley, the hamlet never managed to attain the degree of prosperity enjoyed by other villages hereabouts.

The original church is now merely a slate grey shell, surrounded by the graves of Blawith's past residents. In the year 1782, the residents decided to upgrade their lowly status in the community by having a steeple erected. After selling some poor quality land at Bleas Brow adjoining Coniston Water, the impoverished parishioners were able to complete their project which included the installation of a brand new bell. Scornful comments flowing faster than the infant Crake embodied this satirical ode penned by a less than sympathetic wag:

> *Blawith poor people*
> *An auld church and a new steeple*
> *As poor as hell*
> *They had to sell*
> *A bit of fell*
> *To buy a bell*
> *Blawith poor people!*

Once the old church fell into disrepair, the bell was re-located in the new church down the road apiece. Sadly, unless a miracle occurs, the bell is unlikely to summon the faithful in the foreseeable future due to a declining congregation.

Ruins of the old church at Blawith

The Walk

Before starting out on the walk, an investigation of the old churchyard, now maintained by the local authority, offers an engaging insight into the singular history of this tiny hamlet. Bare stone walls reflect an age when this empty church would have been filled to capacity with parishioners anxious to improve their standing in a thriving community.

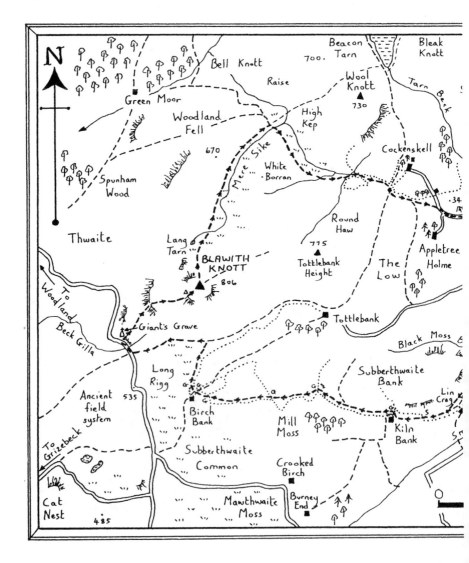

Now take a stroll down to the new church of St John's built in 1883 with its legendary bell on display for all to see. Turn left up the lane opposite which serves the ancient farmstead of Houkler Hall. Fork left up Raisthwaite Lane through a gate next to a bungalow. Then head south-west up the side valley occupied by Smithy Beck through another gate before stopping at the far side of a small wood on the right.

Here join a footpath that has been diverted along the lower edge of the wood between a fence and wall with a new planting of conifers on

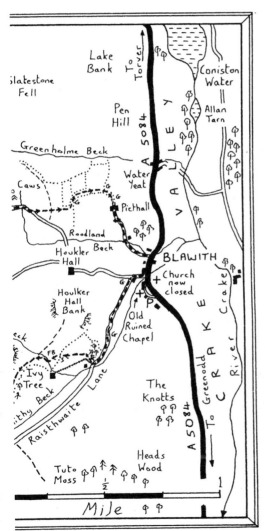

the left. When the trail opens out, bear half left following a line of markers. Beyond a wall stile, drop down to cross Black Moss Beck by a neat slabbed footbridge close to Ivy Tree Farm and thence along a rutted track up the grassy incline of Houkler Hall Bank.

Once above the wall line, watch for a faint path which links the farms around the flank of Subberthwaite Moor. Head left along the upper edge of a wood, past a rusting heap of abandoned farm machinery. No doubt a contemporary artist would make something of this blot on the landscape.

Approaching Lin Crag Farm, take the higher route and then continue alongside the in-take wall. When this climbs Subberthwaite Bank, follow for a brief spell keeping an eagle eye open for the wall stile into the next field and then across to Kiln Bank.

Keep above the farm buildings by accompanying

a fence beyond a gate which will bring you back to the main track. At a fork in the trails, take the left prong along the wall. At the next gate, pay due regard to the fenced outcrop erected to deter recalcitrant sheep from practising their bird impressions. Elements of wool clinging to the barbed strands are evidence of the need for such protection.

Continue west until Birch Bank is reached. Three gates bring you onto the open moorland of Long Rigg. Follow the wall on your right which veers north before circling back towards Tottlebank. Ahead, the noble upthrust of heather clad Blawith Knott issues a mocking challenge that we can but embrace with gusto. Can't we?

Join the clear track heading west from Tottlebank to join the open fell road. Make a right turn, past a clutch of boulders abutting the infant Beck Gila. Another 20 metres will bring you to a clear path ascending the south-west shoulder of Blawith Knott. To the left of the path close to the road, a large flat rock provides the tombstone for what has become known as *The Giant's Grave.*

A depression approximately six feet (2 metres) in length indicates that in the past, such a height would have been regarded with awe when most settlers were of limited stature. Local superstition believes that this particular titan was killed by an arrow fired from some adversary lurking on top of The Knott. Archaeologists, being a less than romantic breed, are apt to claim that such depressions have resulted from the permanent settlement established by Bronze Age man on Subberthwaite Moor.

No bones there now – so strike uphill, the clear trail snaking over a series of rocky knolls to gain the princely apex above. The expansive panorama that opens up is well worth the effort, especially to the north-east where the baronial Old Man of Coniston holds centre stage surrounded by his courtiers.

After paying due homage to the sights on offer from this lofty vantage point, our route lies north-east in the direction of Wool Knott. Ignore the clear trail pointing the way across the tops to Tottlebank Heights. Instead, slant left down a thin trod into the upper reaches of Mire Sike valley head.

This boggy wilderness comprising heather and tough marsh grass is not a favoured locale to break one's leg. Few travellers pass this way and it remains a corner of Lakeland untainted by the hand of man. Populated solely by the spirits of our primitive ancestors, even the stalwart Herdwick seems to have passed it by.

Accompany the unusually dry path along the left side of the shallow vale to meet the main bridleway forging across the Blawith Fells from east to west. Head right along this clear track which makes full use of the pass between Wool Knott and Round Haw. On reaching the in-take wall, the track funnels down a short walled lane before continuing east to join the metalled access road serving Cockenskell.

Bear right along this road for a quarter of a mile keeping watch for a faint left fork just beyond Roodlands Beck. Take a stroll across the open grass common maintaining a straight course to meet a wall which veers left into a dry depression. Pass through a gate to mount the facing bank between walls and through another gate to enter a rough lane. Bear right to reach the group of converted farm buildings known as Picthall.

The metalled access road leads back to the A5084. A quarter of a mile south and we are back at St John's Church. The bell, once a symbol of Blawith's struggle for acceptance within a biased community, now hangs idle and forgotten. Perhaps in the future, an upswing in the fortunes of the parish will again enable the Blawith Bell to evoke a lusty jingle of pride.

20. Murder Most Horrid

Mysteries:	Oxenfell Gate, GR 321019. Betty Yewdale, GR 324034
Distance:	6 miles
Total height climbed:	700 feet/213 metres
Nearest centre:	Elterwater
Start & finish:	Immediately after forking right off the A593 at Skelwith Bridge, park on the left side of the Langdale road. Limited parking is also available after the bridge itself on the left.
Maps:	Ordnance Survey English Lakes, 1:25000, south-east area sheet.

Driving down the A593 towards Skelwith Bridge, the first cluster of stone buildings encountered comprises the hamlet of Clappersgate. Meaning *road over the rough bridge* in old Norse, it was used as a port in the late 18th century from which Langdale slate was loaded onto barges for shipment down Windermere. Far more brisk and energetic than the present sleepy commune, it held regular dances for the locals.

It was here that Betty Briggs attended just such a function with a beau who harboured designs that were not to the young lady's taste. To his chagrin, she chose to dance with a gardener who then offered to escort her back to Tilberthwaite after the dance.

The Walk

Once the River Brathay had been crossed at Skelwith Bridge, the amorous pair turned sharp right up the rising gradient. Like them, we will take the second right-of-way which forks right alongside a fence.

Following behind, his jealous agitation growing more corrosive by the minute, the spurned suitor began to plot his revenge.

Pass through a fence stile to enter a small wood, the path meandering uphill through another stile to the limit of the present tree cover. Beyond the next stile, rolling fields open out towards Langdale and Elterwater. The path heads towards a pair of cottages where a gate allows progress beyond Park House channelled around a high fence with a stile at either end.

At this stage, Jack Slype's insane rage must have been approaching the point of no return as he observed the canoodling couple ahead.

Continue along the wide track to a gate. With a fence on the right, the path circles round to the left into the yard of Park Farm. It now squeezes between two buildings after which a short walk follows with a fence on the left. We soon arrive at the cluster of dwellings that make up Low Park where another pair of stiles must be negotiated.

Slant across the next field towards the wooded coppice overlooking the Brathay. Here the river has cut deeply into the high banking. Enter the woods over yet another stile and descend the winding trail that drops abruptly down to valley level and the exit stile. A short stroll across the flat sward will bring us to the Elterwater road.

In total, fifteen stiles and gates had to be negotiated on this section. In the dark, perhaps the inconvenience did nothing to

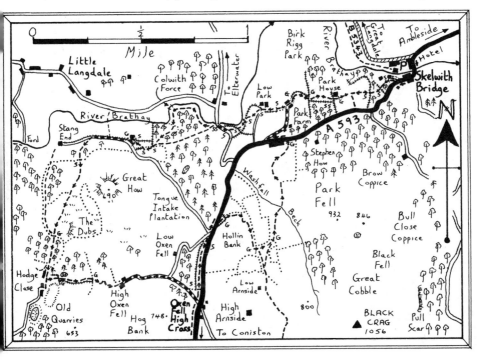

improve the homicidal thoughts rushing through Slype's congealing brain.

Bear right for 50 metres and then enter the northern sector of Tongue Intake Plantation through a double stile. The main route continues ahead towards High Park but we now make a deviation to the right following the river.

Squeezing over the rock bar planted across the entrance to Little Langdale, Colwith Force makes a truculent show of defiance as it pours over the waterfall. Shrugging off the constrictive pressure in the narrow gorge, the river splutters and gurgles under the verdant canopy before resuming its onward course to swell Elterwater downstream.

Had the trio of foot-tappers elected this path, the smouldering Slype might well have exacted retribution in full.

Beyond the Force, strike away from the river through a moss clad section of broken wall climbing gradually to the edge of the plantation. Over a stile, follow the fence on your right to another and then bear right along the farm access track to High Park. Go right behind the farmhouse to emerge onto the road serving Stang End.

Fury beyond compare and the seed of a terminal solution to his dilemma must now have been gnawing at the vitals of the distraught Mr Slype as he staggered along the road in pursuit.

Watch for a signpost on the left indicating the way to Hodge Close. Climb the steep valley side until a wall stile is crossed. The path then heads south skirting a marshy tract between Little Fell and the salient upthrust of Great How on the left. Pass through a gate into the walled enclosure of woodland ahead. Thence continuing onward to Hodge Close at the far side.

Brutalised by torrid thoughts of vengeance, Jack Slype had by now come to a baneful resolution of his plight.

Before the sharp right leading into the main quarry complex, head left past the yawning gulf of an abandoned slate bed. Pass through a gate as the track heads east with a reedy tarn on your left and so across Oxen Fell.

Rapidly closing with his adversary, Slype girded himself for the final denouement.

Arriving at the Oxenfell Gate, the fatal blow was struck. As the gardener lay dead at the feet of a dumbstruck Betty Bragg, the

***killer must have suddenly realised what he had done and imme-
diately took his own life.***

But why would the pair have deviated from the normal route back to
Tilberthwaite? Perhaps they had spotted Slype and, suspecting his
nefarious intentions, hoped to seek assistance at the nearest habitation
which was at High Oxen Fell. In the event they never made it. Each
night, it is said, the shape of a ghostly figure walks this route.

Reflecting on the pangs of this rebuffed admirer, descend a sharp
twist in the trail to reach High Oxen Fell. From this secluded farm
emerged a whimsical tale involving yet another Betty. She was a
Yewdale who lived at Hacket across the north side of Little Langdale.
Capricious and somewhat volatile, she was not one who was easily
hectored.

High Oxen Fell Farm

Brought to prominence by Wordsworth in his epic poem *The Excursion*,
it concerns a funeral attended by her husband. Following the burial
service in Coniston, it was common practice for the male mourners to
toast the memory of the deceased at the local hostelry.

When Jonathan Yewdale failed to return by the next morning, his vexed wife set off to find him. She first called at Oxenfell Farm and there learned that none of the men had yet returned home. Not the most patient of women, Betty descended on the Black Bull spitting fire and brimstone. Jonathan was dragged from the inn with a hazel switch soundly administered by an irate spouse who brandished the stick with the passion of a whirling dervish.

Ashamed at what the neighbours might think of her drink sodden man, she drove him back to Hacket across the fells. The poor fellow was even made to crawl through hog-holes in the dry stone walls as punishment for his sinful debauchery. On the way back, they called at Oxenfell Farm, the farmer's wife graphically describing Jonathan's dishevelled appearance. It is abundantly clear that Betty Yewdale was not a woman to be trifled with.

From the farm, the route is metalled. Fork right after 300 metres dropping down to the main A593 at Oxen Fell High Cross. This marks the highest point of the road before it pursues an amiable descent past Yew Tree Tarn into the Yewdale Valley beyond.

Turn left towards Skelwith Bridge following the path that parallels the left side of the road. After crossing a wall stile, the route thereafter is squeezed between a wall and fence. At the far end, cross the wall and continue walking alongside the road for another 100 metres.

Cross over and fork right up a clear track between a small group of conifers. Beyond the first gate, the track follows a wall on the left. It then circles round to the right crossing a tributary stream and mounting Hollin Bank. Pass through a gate in the wall on the left when the gradient eases. Then accompany another for 200 metres in a westerly direction to meet up with the major track across Arnside Plantation.

Head north through the wall gate along this distinct track as it makes a leisurely descent of Park Fell to the main road. Bear left for 200 metres until the access road for Park Farm is reached. Turn hard right down this lane to the farm and so join up with the outward route. It is then just a matter of retracing your steps back to Skelwith Bridge.

21. Moonshiner Extraordinaire

Mystery:	The Duty Dodger, GR 299032
Distance:	4½ miles
Total height climbed:	1200 feet/366 metres
Nearest centre:	Elterwater
Start & finish:	Take the left fork signposted for Wrynose Pass at the head of Little Langdale. Limited parking is available after 100 metres on the right. Try not to block the rough track used by farm vehicles. Alternatively, continue past Fell Foot and park on the grass verge under the shadow of Castle Howe.
Maps:	Ordnance Survey English Lakes 1:25000, south-west area sheet.

If ever a valley was designed for the convenience of illicit whiskey manufacture, then Little Langdale must rank as a premiere example. Even today with the provision of high powered cars, rarely can the motorist get out of low gear. The narrow road follows a tortuous roller coaster path that endeavours to dissuade onward progression at every turn. Gaining the hallowed Three Shires Stone at the top of Wrynose Pass still remains an achievement worthy of Grade 'A' certification.

It is little wonder, therefore, that such a vale is the preserve of the discerning few who relish the opportunity to wrestle with austere yet magnificently sculpted terrain. What a daunting task it must have been for Excisemen in the last century struggling to catch up with *will o' the wisp* felons, who quickly disappeared with their fiery tipple like a breath of wind. Even the most zealous official must have been disillusioned by the asperity of his chosen profession, particularly in this part of the world.

Most colourful of the clandestine distillers was Lancelot 'Lanty' Slee who began his *spiritual* career at Low Colwith around the middle of the 19th century. A name of Norse origins meaning cunning, clever and sly, this apt derivation could have been initiated with the rascally Lancelot in mind. Stills producing a continuous output of the potent brew were scattered throughout the district to offset unforeseen visits by the revenue-men.

Illicit hooch brewed from locally grown potatoes was much sought after by all elements of the community including magistrates who were not averse to tipping the wink should a raid be in the offing. On the south side of Little Langdale, a still was hidden in one of the old Tilberthwaite quarries. So well concealed were the accoutrements that quarrymen never knew of its existence. Careful investigation of this particular cave which is located in the middle quarry (GR 307024) under Low Fell can 'still' turn evidence of its bizarre past.

Although a tough and resolute character, quick to avenge any slight, the erstwhile moonshiner was highly regarded with customers as far afield as Ravenglass and Kendal. Langdale was a handy base situated as it was at the heart of Lanty's business empire.

Not all raids proved to be fruitless ventures. One such conviction by the Hawkshead magistrates cost the roguish fellow £150 in 1853 which was the equivalent of three years' wages to the ordinary farm labourer. Following this, prospective consumers erred on the side of caution by enquiring if he had harvested 'a good crop of taties this year'.

Age certainly failed to dim the old knave's *spirit* of adventure and he always kept a few stills simmering until his death in 1878. Retiring to Ivy Howe (now known as Iving Howe), he frequently visited one still high above the Langdale Valley close to Red Tarn under the pretext of collecting red haematite ore.

It is perhaps appropriate that this most colourful of Lakeland characters should have spent his final years in the cottage once owned by another celebrated personality who achieved poetic renown as opposed to notoriety. William Wordsworth had bought the property sixty years earlier to sell off the freehold for political gain. His wife Mary described Ivy Howe as "a sweet sunny place with beautiful rocks".

The Walk

From the parking area close to the Blea Tarn fork, continue along the road in the direction of Wrynose Pass. After a quarter of a mile, the narrow winding highway passes the front door of Fell Foot Farm, the well-tended garden being on the opposite side. Directly above the door is an overhanging room supported by pillars and used by Lanty Slee to store copious gallons of his lusty tonic.

Transit of the liquor was assisted by secreting it in pig bladders because of their toughness and ability to distend. One story is told of how the farmer's wife was challenged by Excisemen who suspected Fell Foot of harbouring a cache of the illegal brew. Luckily, she had learned of the impending foray and managed to hide the skins. All that is except for one slung about her person beneath a voluminous skirt.

Vigorously berating the officers as they searched the premises, it was fortunate indeed that they failed to include her in the probing scrutiny. Although suspicious in the extreme, the representatives of the law were forced to accede that their informant had on this occasion been mistaken. No doubt Lanty and his buxom colleague enjoyed a few noggins in celebration; hence the origin of the saying *to have a skinful* which denotes an over-indulgence of the amber nectar.

As you walk past Fell Foot, the road begins to climb, the view ahead being dominated by the rocky excrescence of Castle Howe. Now providing a lofty perch from which to admire the majestic tone of the valley, it is easy to realise what a first rate observation post it would have made in less tranquil times. In addition to keeping watch for the approach of Excisemen, wandering bands of itinerant beggars were also a threat to consider.

Behind Fell Foot is to be found a rectangular flat-topped mound

Fell Foot – illicit whiskey was stored in the room above the doorway

thought to be the rendezvous for important Viking council meetings. Known as a *thing-mount*, the site played a vital role in the management of early Norse affairs during that turbulent epoch. Barely recognisable following centuries of agricultural change, archaeologists still work up a rigorous sweat when faced with this singular relic of local government in medieval Cumbria.

Walk past Castle Howe for approximately 200 metres keeping an eye open for a clear passageway through the bracken collar on the right. Negotiate a short tract of marshy ground to cross the small tributary of Bleamoss Beck. Locate a distinct track on the far side which climbs to join the main right-of-way from the Wrynose road. Bear right following this towards the scooped hollow occupied by Blea Tarn. Beyond the noble upthrust of Tarnclose Crag, cross a stile to the pine-fringed west bank of the tarn.

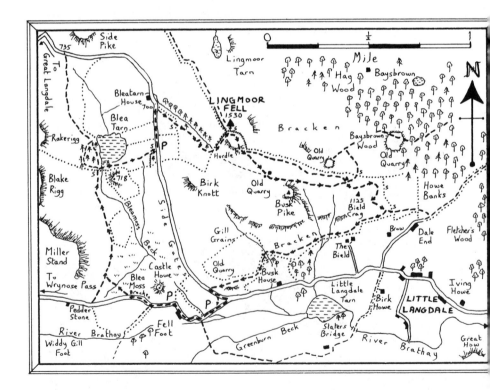

Formed by ice overflowing from the main Langdale glacier, Blea Tarn is the jewel in the crown. Cross the footbridge and tread a newly laid path that points unerringly to the road joining the twin valleys. Turn left opposite the car-park heading along the road towards the isolated settlement of Blea Tarn House.

Directly ahead, a knobbly chunk of bare rock assumes the appearance of a miniature Pike o' Stickle. Although lacking in altitude, Side Pike packs a sting in the tail if not handled with care. It marks the north-west extremity of Lingmoor Fell, a parabolic mass of distinctive green slate which is still quarried at Elterwater. Keep Side Pike in mind for a future visit.

Blea Tarn House has been eulogised by the eloquent pen of William Wordsworth in his epic poem *The Excursion*. Today, the occupant referred to as 'The Solitary', would feel sadly out of place around Blea Tarn in what has become a tourist honeypot.

Wordsworth was one of the early pioneer fell wanderers to explore the Lake District and write a detailed guide on his travels. Frequently covering more than thirty miles in a single day, he championed the maintenance of public footpaths writing *The Excursion* as a secret yearning for the simple life of the roving itinerant.

Before the kink in the road at the farm, head left up the fell path alongside a tree-girt ravine. More than likely, this is the route Wordsworth took to ascend Lingmoor Fell whilst composing his pensive ode in 1814. Pathless in those days, today a distinct trod guides the modern hiker initially over a new wall stile up the steepening ridge. A series of zigzags passing through a cemetery of decayed tree-stumps leads one to the head of the gully amidst a sconce of larches.

Cross the wall by a hurdle and bear left alongside a disintegrating wall and more recent fence. A brief climb brings us to the summit of Lingmoor Fell gained across the fence by a stile.

No more impressive station to savour the topography of Greater Langdale is available than that enjoyed from this lofty grandstand. The unique moulding of the Langdale Pikes across the valley has been a photographer's dream for generations, the chiselled amplitude being readily picked out even from across Morecambe Bay.

Enjoy this unequivocal Lakeland skyline to the full before re-crossing the fence to head south-east along the main ridge. Our route slants away from the fence once it becomes a wall to descend a stony bank aiming for the cluster of ruined quarry buildings below. Fork right off the main path to follow a narrow trod down into the broad shelf strewn with abandoned slate paraphernalia.

Continue south-east along the miner's access track passing the gnarled protuberance of Busk Pike on the right. Upon reaching an obvious walkers' cross-roads, take the right arm past a large cairn topping Bield Crag. Meandering through the bracken, the path descends the steeply shelving southern flank into Little Langdale. Well-graded to accommodate the transport of finished slate using a series of tacks, the track merges with the old Elterwater link close to Dale End.

Before this track passes through a wall, veer right along the upper edge of the valley in-take wall. Passing beneath the frost shattered cliffs of Bield Crag, it is a poignant reminder that this is where the ill-fated shepherd in *The Excursion* plummeted to his doom whilst searching for a lost sheep. Whether this inclusion was based on fact has not been clarified. As you follow the narrow path under the louring crags, it requires little imagination to appreciate the dangers above.

Descending this enjoyable and little known trail past The Bields, our route eventually arrives at a rock step across the unnamed ravine above Busk House. Swing left through a gate and make your way around the lower slopes of Gill Grains on a grassy shelf. The path then descends to the Blea Tarn road where we turn left to complete the walk.

22. Don't Call the Ferryman

Mystery:	The Crier of Claife, GR 386982
Distance:	6 miles
Total height climbed:	900 feet/273 metres
Nearest centre:	Far Sawrey
Start & finish:	Ash Landing National Trust Car Park, located in a clearing below Red Brow on the approach to the ferry.
Maps:	Ordnance Survey English Lakes, 1:25000, south-east area sheet.

Having the distinction of being England's largest lake has meant that Windermere's overall length of ten miles is impossible to negotiate by road vehicles. Since earliest times, a ferry has plied across the narrowest point, a distance of a quarter of a mile between The Nab on the eastern shore and a promontory at the terminus of the current B 5285.

Once merely a rowing boat, passengers were required to hail the ferryman by calling "*Boat! Boat!*" One such summons on an equally windswept night back in the 16th century was ignored by some of the carousing boatmen who were in fear of the legendary *Crier of Claife*. Lurking amidst the tree clad slopes of the Heights, this infamous spectre was reputed to lure unsuspecting travellers to their doom.

The continued cry for assistance was finally answered by a mild mannered fellow who scoffed at the timidity of his colleagues. Not returning in the usual time for a crossing, the others went outside to search for him. Eventually found on the shore with an empty boat, the distraught ferryman had been terrorised into a stunned silence. What happened to the luckless oar-puller was never discovered as he died mysteriously a few days later.

Over the next few months, the *Crier of Claife* clearly must have been hungry for more victims judging by his vociferous output. But nobody responded, even when the calls were from genuine passengers. In consequence, business suffered to such an extent that local tradesmen felt that something should be done to dissolve the influence of the malevolent wraith forever.

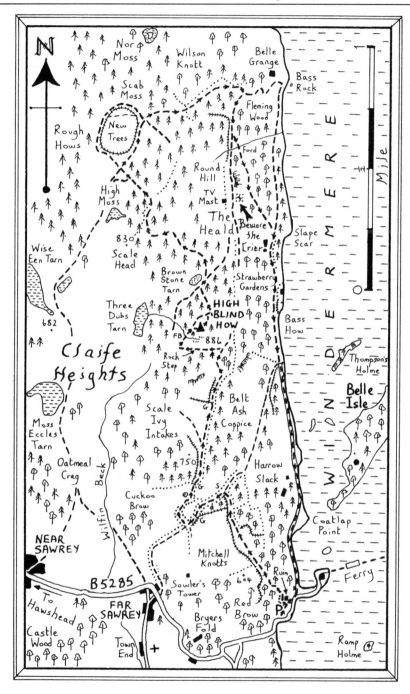

A monk from Furness Abbey was sent for to exorcise the spirit. On Christmas Day, following a particularly poignant service, the congregation ascended a track up to a remote quarry on the steep slopes overlooking Windermere. Here it was that the *Crier of Claife* was entombed with the lasting acclamation that this unholy spectre should remain until "dryshod men walk on Winander and trot their ponies through solid crags."

And that should have seen an end to the nefarious deeds of this boggle (a malignant spirit). Yet still he is credited with certain unexplained happenings.

Why do foxhounds stop dead near Crier Quarry refusing to continue the hunt? What became of the Colthouse schoolmaster who came to investigate the legend and was never seen again? Was it the *Crier* who had a hand in the drowning of forty-seven guests returning from a marriage ceremony on the far shore when their overloaded craft sunk beneath them?

One story published in the Westmorland Gazette of August 1891 suggests that the *Crier* is the spirit of a monk who fell in love with a French singer. For besmirching his celibate vows, the poor fellow was excommunicated and now walks the Heights above Sawrey. Sightings of a ghostly figure clad in a grey habit have been reported from time to time.

Perhaps you, dear reader, may discover the answer to this sinister mystery, if perchance you amass the courage to trespass within the domain of the *Crier of Claife Heights*.

The Walk

Enter the woods below Red Brow direct from the car park and make your way up a gentle rise to a rock stairway. The climb zigzags up to a ruined summer house dating from the 18th century which was constructed by the Curwens of Belle Isle. Used as a viewing station by guests at the Ferry House, a sumptuous hotel until 1939, it was described at the time as "a tower with windows of variously coloured glass, through which the landscape appears by turns in the garb of all the seasons". Unfortunately, only the bare skeleton now remains.

During World War II, the Ferry House was occupied by an art school under the trusteeship of the Curwen estate. Since 1947, the premises have been owned by the Freshwater Biological Association founded to investigate the ecology of Windermere and its environs.

Continue past and up a rough trail waymarked by white flashes. Upon reaching a fence, head right along the edge of Mitchell Knotts. After some small distance, the path drops slightly away from the fence before entering a corridor between wall and fence. At the end, cross a stile to a major walled lane.

Turn left, accompanying the lane round through a gate. At the next gate, bear sharp right following the lane past a small tarn on the left. Keep with this obvious route, with the wall on your right through two more gates to enter a constricted passage. At the end of this, the path climbs steeply through the bracken into the dense heart of conifers.

At a break of trail marked by a signpost, head due west towards Hawkshead across a dank carpet of discarded pine needles. Deathly silent, gnarled roots like squirming tentacles attempt to inveigle the unwary traveller as he negotiates the gloomy trail. Again, it is the frequent splashes from white markers that point the way like cat's eyes on a road.

Watch for a rock step at the edge of an open glade interspersed with exposed tors. Following an abrupt right angle, the path re-enters the tree-cover, dropping down to cross a marshy clearing on a short foot-bridge. Beyond, the path climbs through a murky tunnel of firs to emerge on the apex of Claife Heights which has been cleared.

The summit of High Blind How is easily missed. So before the descent to the forest beyond, climb right to locate the trig column ensconced within bracken and mounted on a rock dais. A hundred metres to the north-east, a flat sward of cropped turf with slate intrusions provides the ideal resting place for lunch whilst imbibing the perspective across Windermere. Identifying the distant peaks whilst chomping on your butties makes for a thoroughly congenial sojourn.

Merge back into the main track and drop down to a T-junction near the rim of trees where a left turn is made. The path soon forks into a wide forest road where we head to the right. After 100 metres at the far end of Brown Stone Tarn, leave the road on your left to climb into the verdant screen at the far side.

After passing across a rock slab where the dense foliage again thins to reveal an open prospect, pause to survey the far shore before plunging back into the woody soup. Dropping down, the path homes into an old moss-shrouded wall and follows it for a brief spell. When the wall

The summit of High Blind How on Claife Heights

finally disintegrates, bear left heading north-west past a forest track on the left and up to a walkers' cross-roads.

Take the right arm accompanying a high fence on the left which protects new conifers from the rapacity of young deer. Much of this area known as Long Height has been cleared and, as with all similar despoliation, is ugly in the extreme until new plantings take hold. After a quarter of a mile, we come to a major forest road and immediately cross straight over into an old tract of mixed woodland signposted to Belle Grange.

Clearly defined, the path begins to descend this eastern flank of Claife Heights known as the Heald. After making a hard right, the breast route back to Far Sawrey climbs back to the right. At this point, decisions have to be made as to whether you wish to err on the side of caution and not tempt the devil's messenger. Should this be your chosen course of action, by all means continue down-slope to Belle Grange and return along the shore trail alongside Windermere with a clear conscience. And who could blame you?

Hardy souls wishing to test the metal of the *Crier* in his own arena should drink deep from the cup of knowledge before setting forth to rub shoulders with this legendary denizen. Exorcised he may be, but who can say how long such a protection will last.

A brief climb up the stony track will bring you to another deer fence on the right. Soon thereafter, break left down a clear path which descends through the tree cover passing under the threatening overhang of an exposed crag called Round Hill.

Just beyond, the old quarry is reached wherein the spirit of the *Crier of Claife* is imprisoned. Anger and frustration with his enforced constraint are evident from the chaotic splay of boulders strewn about amongst the trees.

No birds chirrup and cavort in this dark brooding place. Clutching branches with a life of their own reach out to enfold you in their moody clasp. But this is no Vincent Price movie. If a sudden chill runs down your spine like the numbing hand of death, maybe you also have felt the presence of *The Crier*.

A masochistic temptation to linger should be resisted. Instead, hurry down to the palliative shores of Lake Windermere and the civilising influence of the 20th century. After all, ghosts are only a figment of an overactive imagination – aren't they?

Opposite the north end of Belle Isle, a cattle grid marks where the right-of-way becomes metalled. The large island practically blocks off the upper end of Windermere and is a favourite destination for casual visitors arriving by rowing boat. Barely visible through a sheltering screen of trees, the imposing house erected thereon is open to the public. It is unusual in being the first dwelling in Britain to be of round construction and has been in the Curwen Family for over two centuries.

Built in 1774 for a Mr Graham, he later sold it at a considerable loss after friends ridiculed the unorthodox design. Attractive gardens were laid out by Isabella Curwen, who changed the original name from Longholme. John Curwen incurred the wrath of Wordsworth by planting over one million larches on the Heights. The venerable poet was much offended by "an introduction of discordant objects, disturbing that peaceful harmony of form and colour, which had been through a long lapse of ages most happily preserved".

Virtually flat, Belle Isle was submerged following a torrential downpour in November of 1958 when it was possible to row across the island between the trees poking out of the eddying reach. Another prestigious event for Belle Isle was the distinction of hosting the first Lakeland sheep dog trials in 1877 which took place "before a large and fashionable gathering".

On reaching the ferry road, turn left towards Far Sawrey for 100 metres. Take the second gap in the wall on your right to make use of a woodland trail back to the car park.

Since time immemorial, the ferry has provided a vital link across Windermere, and is still a well-utilised local amenity. On a fine day when sunlight dapples the gently rippling swell, the *Crier of Claife* becomes just a quirky tale related to liven up ferry crossings. But when storm clouds threaten, and swirling mist wraps a saturnine cloak around the verdant ranks blanketing The Heald, every freakish sound assumes a sinister intent. Who will then deny the *Crier* his right to immortality? Certainly not I.

23. Copper Load Of This!

Mysteries:	Simon's Nick, GR 281989. Levers Water, GR 279994
Distance:	5½ miles
Total height climbed:	1250 feet/380 metres
Nearest centre:	Coniston
Start & finish:	A pull-in on the right just beyond the Church of the Sacred Heart at Bowmanstead which lies three-quarters of a mile south from Coniston village on the A593.
Maps:	Ordnance Survey English Lakes 1:25,000, south-west area sheet.

In similar vein to Hawkshead, the old established mining enclave of Coniston has long regarded itself as having the prestigious honorarium of town status. The degree of prosperity realised from the exploitation of rich copper ore secreted deep within the bowels of the Coniston Fells, ensured a permanence that continues to this day.

Transport was the key and the arrival of the eight mile branch line from the main Furness Railway in 1859 enabled copper ore to be exported faster and in larger quantities than before. Such a testament to the importance of the town within the industrial province cannot be understated. Although doubtless at the time, the possibilities for a stimulation of tourist traffic were not overlooked.

After 1890 when most of the mining had ceased, the railway had to rely solely on tourists until its final demise in 1957. Today, the line is barely recognisable as such, most visitors never having seen the station which is tucked away above the town, a redundant vestige of a bygone era.

The Walk

Our walk begins close to the route of the old railway which parallels the main road. Stroll back towards Coniston for 50 metres and take the narrow lane alongside the Church of the Sacred Heart. This passes beneath the line which has now been dismantled. Turn immediately right to follow the steep access road serving a row of four cottages.

Thereafter, the way continues in its original rough state. After clearing three gates, watch for a gate on the right.

Head north across the field through another gate to reach Heathwaite. Here, our route passes to the right of the farm buildings where the resident sheep dog clearly prefers the tickling attention from humans than engaging in its normal agrarian duties. Continue beyond the farm using a distinct track which meets the fell road rising from Coniston at a z-bend. Ahead and 100 metres further, the path resumes by following a wall and then dropping down into the tributary valley of Scrow Beck.

Cross the beck by way of a footbridge swinging right under the looming charge of Foul Scrow. The thin trail slants round into the main valley cut by Church Beck. Make a gradual descent of this steep south-west flank of the valley to merge with the principal track from Coniston adjacent to the Miners' Bridge. Downstream, Church Beck presents a rampaging torrent of erosive power. On the far side, bear left along the rough mine road to enter Coppermines Valley itself.

The extent of man's despoliation of the landscape in his quest for metal is patently obvious. A veritable cornucopia of industrial relics abounds to wet the appetite of the most critical archaeologist. As the

Main entrance to the underground labyrinth of Coppermines Valley

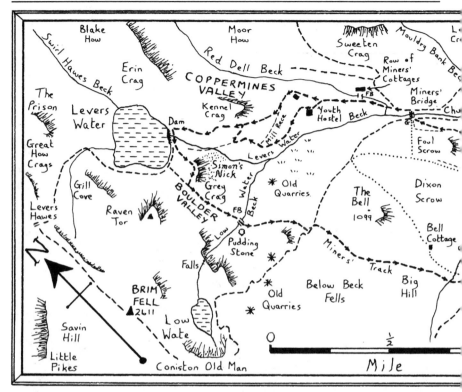

mine office (now a popular youth hostel) is neared, huge spoil tips rise up complementing the abandoned paraphernalia of this once bustling corner of Lakeland.

In 1830, almost one thousand men were employed in the mines. Sweating in the cramped levels to extract the precious ore required prodigious nerve and a strong back. Many of the adits driven deep into the steep hillsides are still accessible today although highly dangerous for the novice who should maintain a respectable distance. Accidents and loss of life were a constant threat to all who ventured underground, such that the devil himself was reckoned to inhabit the maze of subterranean galleries.

Certainly in the mid 19th century, a Mrs Linton felt that malevolent forces were in control of the mine workings. She described in eloquent prose her fears regarding the "*bogies, kobolds, gnomes and all manner of evil influences in the very entrails of the Old Man*".

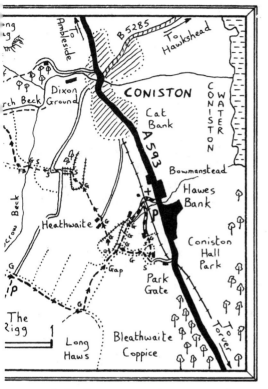

To some, the frenetic turmoil that characterises Coppermines Valley has no place in the plan for a modern National Park and should be swept clean or drowned under an artificial reservoir along with the ghostly myths. A valid option but one that ignores a past that established itself aeons before achieving NP status. Such a choice would be to erase a vibrant part of the area's heritage.

Those who seek an easy alternative up to Levers Water should stick with the mine road all the way. Intrepid adventurers will fork right up to the restored accommodation block, circling above and behind to locate the lower mill race. Originally used as conduits for transporting water, they make excellent pathways for the modern day explorer.

Take note of the black hole straight ahead on the far side of Red Dell Beck where it plunges down from the hanging valley above. This noxious orifice marks the main entrance to the underground labyrinth. Cheerless and repellent, especially when approached under the oppressive canopy of a darkening sky, could this be the gateway to hell itself? Only the Devil's Disciples and foolhardy yokels will seek admittance.

Wiser mortals should slant uphill away from the lower mill race to locate an obscure path connecting with the upper race. Accompany this on a clear grass path around the shoulder of Tongue Brow until it merges with the stony track which terminates at Levers Water.

As height is gained, a cataclysmic split in the cliff face on the opposite side of the valley dominates the near horizon. Nobody can deny the awesome mould of this rabid slice hacked from bare rock by the hand of some primeval Cyclops. There is little doubt that the bronze-streaked cleft known as Simon's Nick has the Devil's mark indelibly branded upon it.

The story is told of how Simon, a local miner, struck a rich vein of copper and claimed that fairies had directed him to the auspicious site. Others who knew the lucky fellow were less than charitable by suggesting that Lucifer himself was the guiding hand.

Over the next few months, Simon was unable to consolidate his holding and suffered a series of strange misfortunes. Claim robbers and frequent accidents finally resulted in the poor chap being blown up by his own gunpowder, whether by accident or design was never established. But since that ill-fated occurrence, the apparition of Simon is said to haunt the vicinity of the yawning fissure. Climbers hanging like spiders to the rock face have espied the wraithlike figure lurking amidst the debris strewn within the confines of the Nick.

Once the broad corrie occupied by Levers Water is reached, cross the beck to mount an easy grass slope. On your right is the dam which artificially raised the level of the tarn to provide additional water for the smelting process down valley. The true character of the deep copper vein soon becomes apparent along with other levels in the area. Great care is essential if a premature appointment with Simon is to be avoided.

Without question, a close encounter with the grandiose rift remains the high point of this walk in many ways. To the north, Levers Water has also achieved a certain notoriety amongst fishermen, some of whom are sure it contains an immense hairy trout which is said to be "*bigger than man had ever seen*".

Descend the gentle slope to reach the col below Raven Tor. Then turn left to follow a clear trail down into the appropriately designated Boulder Valley. Cross Low Water Beck on a footbridge marvelling at the silver winged cascades bubbling forth from the hidden corrie tarn of Low Water above.

Dominating the shallow depression is the Pudding Stone, a monstrous off-cut wrested from the craggy heights above. What an inspirational experience for Stone Age Johnny to have witnessed as he chipped away at his flint axe-heads – provided of course he was outside the drop zone.

Big as a house, the Pudding Stone is simple to climb and makes for an exhilarating perch. King of Boulders, this stalwart Goliath might not have achieved the renown of its Borrowdale cousin, but such a remote site ensures you a degree of seclusion that should be savoured to the full.

Head south-east out of this giant's rockery to meet the quarry road descending from the Old Man. Turn left and follow the rough trail down past The Bell to the start of Walna Scar. Continue across and accompany the in-take wall on your left. The narrow yet clear path makes an obvious left swing through a gate after a quarter of a mile heading down a field parallel to a small gill.

Funnelling into a walled corridor, it passes through a gap and down to a cramped lane on the right. Follow this tree-lined conduit through a gate thence keeping an eye open for a wooden stile on the left. This indicates a newly created route alternative avoiding the houses at Park Gate. Aim north-east for a slab stile in the field corner enabling you to pass right of Spoon Hall. Through the next gate, it is but a short stroll down the metalled access road back to the main highway.

The dangers of hard rock mining experienced by the mysterious Simon and his contemporaries are all too apparent when viewed at close quarters. Many of the shafts and adits are flooded, others are in imminent danger of collapse. Ensure that his fate is not yours by erring on the side of caution at all times.

24. No Place to Hang About

Mystery:	Gibbet Hill, GR 624994
Distance:	6 miles
Total height climbed:	1600 feet/488 metres
Nearest centre:	Tebay
Start & finish:	Approaching from the south along the old Roman highway known as Fairmile Road, there is ample parking space on the broad swathe of grass just before dropping down to cross Carlingill Bridge.
Maps:	Ordnance Survey 1:25000 Pathfinder, Sedbergh and Baugh Fell.

Now completely given over to wandering woollies and the occasional walker, it is difficult to conceive that in the last century, a popular annual fair was held on the grassy tract known as the Fair Mile. Then a major thoroughfare along the Lune Valley, it attracted a host of ne'er-do-wells.

A previous era had witnessed the passage of Roman legions bent on subduing the dissolute Brigantean tribes of the North. They were based at the fort of Alauna located two miles north of Carlin Gill in a strategic position controlling the entrance to the Lune Gorge.

More sinister by far were the perverse activities of a group of miscreants led by one William Smurthwaite during the later years of the 17th century. All that now remains to mark the skulduggery appropriated to this rascally upstart is a name on the Ordnance Survey map just south of Carlingill Bridge. Here it was that the bandit leader took a gruesome finale on what became known as Gibbet Hill.

But Smurthwaite was no common footpad. Attaining the rank of High Constable for Lonsdale, and juror at the Kendal Quarter Sessions, he nevertheless succumbed to the felonious temptations he was sworn to prosecute. Rampant theft and burglary throughout the district were committed by the gang together with the hanging offence of *coin clipping*. This latter involved the paring of silver coins to melt the metal down and so produce illegal coinage.

Following a series of crimes, the motley crew were arrested in 1683 and charged with sixteen offences, many of which carried the death penalty. They were brought before the Appleby Assizes for trial and, much to the dismay and anger of the local populace, were acquitted. Boasting openly of their villainous deeds and cocking a snook at the law, it was inevitable that sooner or later the robber band led by William Smurthwaite and his brother George would cook their goose.

So it was that on the 16th August 1684, the infamous Hanging Judge Jeffries sentenced the notorious duo to be hanged by the neck until dead at Lancaster Castle. Being the leader, it was William's body that was incarcerated in a metal cage and strung up to rot along the Fairmile Road on Gibbet Hill. There he remained as a warning to others of similar ilk as to the fate that would ensue should they be so minded.

The Walk

Our walk begins at the site where Smurthwaite was hung up, now a lonely desolate place. The initial phase of the walk accompanies the impressive valley of Carlin Gill, deep into the core of the Howgill Massif and along the edge of the Yorkshire Dales National Park. On the ground there is no indication of this northern limit and it remains a confounding mystery to me, at least, as to why the boundary line was made to cut across the middle of these graceful mounds.

Barely discernible from the road, one of the most spectacular ravines in the northern fell country awaits the discerning fell-wanderer. A mind boggling conjunction of gladiatorial forces have battled to ensure that here is presented a special corner of the Howgills known only to the sagacious few. Awesome in its intensity, The Spout, an outstanding 30 foot cataract, is second only in the quality of its scenic value to the mighty Dungeon Ghyll in Great Langdale.

From Carlingill Bridge, accompany the beck on its right bank along a thin trod which sticks close to the valley floor but above the level of the flood plain. Meandering across water cut river terraces, the beck is hemmed in between steeply shelving grass flanks. Beyond Small Gill, the valley narrows appreciably as the path crosses to the far side and the heart quickens as excitement quickly mounts in the fervid anticipation of what is to come.

Criss-crossing the bed of the watercourse is necessary depending on the level of water. In periods following heavy rainfall, when the power and volume of water increase substantially, progress up the ravine may be severely curtailed. If this is the case, a higher level path on the south

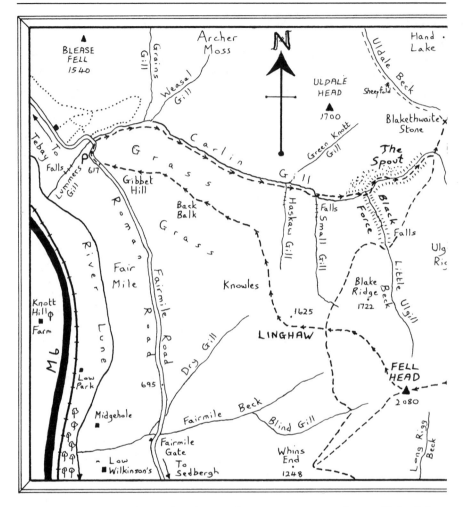

flank is recommended. Clearly, it is better to attempt this walk in drier conditions to enjoy the full benefit offered by The Spout.

After the initial taster, the dramatic gash of Black Force is exposed in all its baleful splendour, a gargantuan rent of shattered rock carved out with devastating effect by Little Ulgill Beck. These inspiring and grandiose surroundings are hidden from casual view and can only be reached by intrepid explorers imbued with a sense of adventure.

If conditions allow, continue up the rock strewn gorge sticking close to the spirited vigour of the beck to savour the full majesty of the

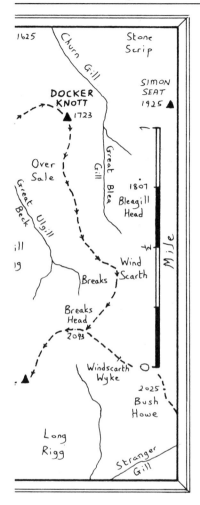

occasion until you arrive at The Spout. Pouring over the lip in undiluted fury, the cascade closely rivals its more eminent colleague at Cautley Spout on the eastern fringe of the Howgills. Our present locale, however, is infinitely preferable being secluded and largely unknown.

To escape a drenching, climb the grassy bank on the left before returning to the stream and an easier gradient above. Soon thereafter, the main beck swings away to the south-east as it debouches from the upper reaches of Breaks. Here, we join a clear track forking in from the right. Continue ahead into the amphitheatre marked by the diminutive Blakethwaite Stone, a watershed between the drainage to north and south.

Strike up the short though steep eastern slope, bearing right onto the neat summit of Docker Knott surmounted by a cairn of minuscule proportions. Head south around the left side of Over Scale above the deep valley head of Great Blea Gill. Aim for a clear path ahead that ascends the broad grassy ridge of Taffergill Hill. The path fades as Wind Scarth is neared but another is soon joined slanting right to merge with the main prime circuit of the Howgill fell tops at Breaks Head.

This major footway sweeping round from The Calf heads south-west onto the summit of Fell Head, easily recognised from afar by its own integral flag pole. The subsidiary top is slightly lower and askew from the main route. From this lofty perch, the whole expanse of the Lune Gorge can be appreciated to the full. A vibrant and essential gap in the northern fells, it has stimulated the flow of traffic since Roman times when the Fairmile Road was the principal artery.

Head north down Blake Ridge on a faint path, aiming left to cross a narrow but distinctive col up the facing slope of Linghaw. This broad featureless sward has no pronounced summit of merit in view of the dearth of rocks needed to construct a cairn. The western slopes do, however, provide an excellent launch pad for hang gliders which can often be seen circling on the rising thermals.

Maintain a north-westerly course above Carlin Gill, picking up a clear trail over Back Balk that leads unerringly down to the road. Don't be overawed at the presence of numerous rough looking fell ponies that frequent these lonely fells, they are herbivores and unlikely to regard you as a succulent morsel for lunch.

The exact location of the gibbet upon which William Smurthwaite danced with the devil is in doubt. Suffice it to say that such a vision acted as a salutary warning to all who passed this way that criminals could expect no mercy from the law. On dark days when a cloying mist eddied about these remote fells and the wind howled its sad lament, no more terrifying sight could be imagined.

25. The Spirit of Kendal

Mysteries:	Angel Inn, GR 515926. The Wildman Ghost, GR 519931
Distance:	9½ miles
Total height climbed:	1100 feet/335 metres
Start & finish:	At weekends, free parking is available on the council office car park on the right of the Windermere road, 100 metres north of Dandes Avenue.
Maps:	Ordnance Survey English Lakes, 1:25000, south-east area sheet.

Often referred to as *The Gateway to the Lakes*, many visitors now avoid Kendal all together since the new by-pass was constructed. In so doing, they miss out on the most fascinating of Lakeland towns. Steeped in historical tradition with much of it still visible to the observant eye, any time spent following the town trail of Arthur Nicholls is well worth a couple of days from anybody's vacation.

Three castle sites within the town's environs must rank as a unique feature unmatched elsewhere. Unless, of course, you know different. From the era of Roman occupation when the fort at Alava occupied a defensive position on a loop of the River Kent, the town has grown to its current dominance of south-east Cumbria.

Originally prospering from the wool trade, Kendal has recently celebrated 800 years as a fully chartered market town with all the prestige such a heritage confers. Flemish weavers settled here from the 14th century producing a heavy cloth that became known as *Kendal Green*. Is it any wonder that the town's motto is **Wool is my Bread**? Legend suggests that the famous hue was produced by blending yellow gorse flowers with blue woad. Certainly Henry VIII favoured the material introduced to him by the town's most eminent daughter who became his sixth wife.

Perhaps the most obvious feature that separates Kendal from its contemporaries regarding individuality are the 'burgage' plots along either side of the main street. Narrow yards connected by alleys provided housing for the town's poorest citizens and are still very noticeable today. Most were squalid unsanitary affairs unlike the picturesque conversions that draw smiles of admiration from today's visitors. There are 150 yards in all, most named after the burgage owner.

Many people assume that the true purpose of the yards was for defence. Once the outer door was closed, the residents would be protected from pillaging raiders sweeping down from the North. Truth of the matter is that cheap housing was needed for the influx of workers in the burgeoning woollen industry of the late 18th century. Land was at a premium between the steep fell side and the river bottom, so high density infilling occurred.

It is indeed a fact that much of the urban growth that stretches up the fell to the west of Stricklandgate was a breeding ground for diseases such as cholera and typhoid. Plagues rampaged through the overcrowded tenements. In 1598, one epidemic devastated a third of the town's population who were said to have been buried in a mass grave on Scout Scar. Only the maze of narrow ginnels remains to tantalise the curious explorer.

The Walk

Our walk starts by turning right up Maude Street by the traffic lights at the northern end of Stricklandgate. Enter Noble's Rest which is a park dedicated to quiet reflection by the wife of Samuel Clark Noble, a local dignitary who died in 1929. A huge block of pink granite dominates the grassy sward.

Aim for the far left corner where a paved walkway leads out onto a narrow back lane known as Low Fellside. Take a stroll south past the premises of the most famous confectionery in the mountaineering fraternity. Quiggins Mint Cake is considered essential nibbling on most British expeditions and enjoys an international market.

About 50 metres short of All Hallows Lane, turn sharp right up Sepulchre Lane. Steeply cobbled, here is a taste of the *auld grey town* as it once appeared. Bogbles have been heard to come charging down this lane creating a disturbance "like a cartload of stones being unloaded." Step aside quickly lest you be trampled in the flurry.

On the left is a Quaker graveyard. Austere and lacking ostentation as befitted the Society of Friends, the Sepulchre was bought in 1656 for the princely sum of £9.30. A welcome patch of greenery amidst the silvery grey limestone that characterises local architecture, this is no place for us to tarry so early on this walk.

Continue up the hillside to Cliff Brow, a narrow ginnel on the left which is now stepped for easy movement up the steep cant. Side cobbling gives some indication of the original composition of this area where such ginnels festooned the area. All available space was built upon giving Fellside a Dickensian aura.

At its far end, the passage assumes the rough cobbled texture of its colourful past. Turn right into Serpentine Road for 100 metres thence slanting left into Queens Road. Another 100 metres will bring you to the start of the fell track on the left.

At the commencement of the right-of-way which is paved initially, enter Serpentine Wood through a pinched wall gap. Follow the clear trail, soon branching left into the heart of the woodland and passing left of a well set like a jewel in the limestone clasp. Keep left at the next junction up to a low crag. Strike up by the side of this natural wall to arrive close to the western edge of the wood. Abutting the golf course, head north past a small building that on closer inspection turns out to be an old lime kiln.

Make your way to the top edge of Serpentine Wood and exit through another small gap onto the open fell overlooking north Kendal. Bear left alongside the wall to the edge of the golf course. An official right-of-way crosses the links maintaining a west north-westerly bearing. But keep an eye out for attacks from low flying golf balls.

Keep right of the highest point and a clump of conifers on the horizon. This will bring you to a wall skirting Kettlewell Crag. This has been demolished for 100 metres to enable golfing to continue down the spur of Helsfell Nab.

Our route heads north-west alongside the continuing wall across two stiles down towards the by-pass. Cross the footbridge into the field beyond turning immediately right and over another wall stile. Thereafter, the route maintains a direct course to the corner of the field. Another stile is followed by a simple stroll up to the substantial cairn on top of Cunswick Fell.

Should a grey mantle of cloud descend to cast a gloomy shadow across the bare fell, do not be surprised to witness the fleeting passage of a spectre from the past that is known to haunt the Scar. This would be the ghost of Roger de Leyburne who stabbed his father in the back to gain control of the Cunswick estate. Such a dastardly action was bound to backfire. Sure enough, one night soon after, the hooded figure of a priest was seen to enter Roger's chamber without emerging. Next day, the culprit was discovered with a knife in his side.

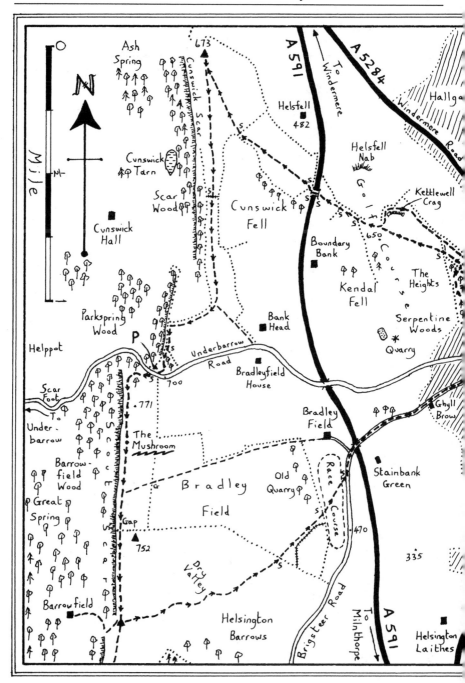

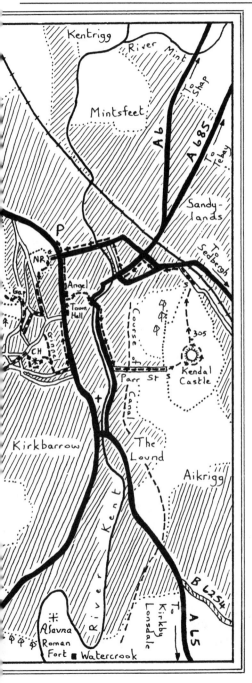

The gently shelving approach to Cunswick Fell from the east gives no indication of the dramatic limestone scaring above the Lyth Valley. This abrupt downfall into the tree clad fringe is both unexpected and dangerous to the unwary traveller. When viewed from Whitbarrow across the valley, the rugged grandiosity of the escarpment presents a thrilling tableau to the eye.

Cunswick Scar is oddly set back from its neighbour Scout Scar for a quarter of a mile on a new fault line. Head due south down an easy slope into a depression before the path rises between constricting parallel walls. Pass over a fence stile continuing ahead until a signpost is reached where the old fell road known as Gamblesmire Lane is crossed.

Bear right to follow a permissive footpath alongside the wall until it reaches the wood at the end of Cunswick Scar which is dominated by a radio mast. Keep to the right side of the wood to emerge above an old quarry now resurrected as a car park. Cross Underbarrow Road and through an iron kissing gate to climb round onto the exposed upper fell of Scout Scar where tree growth is somewhat restricted. Mounds of silvery grey limestone mingle with the heather and tough moorland grass.

But it is *The Mushroom* that holds centre stage on this windswept plateau. Set back from the rim of the escarpment, this man made edifice was erected in 1912 to the lasting memory of King George V. Unequalled as a viewpoint, a crosswall shelter supports the domed roof. Painted on the inside is the distant horizon with landmarks noted for easy recognition.

A unique visual indicator, *The Mushroom* does not, however, occupy the officially recognised summit. This honour lies half a mile to the south hidden by a broken wall. Slightly lower by a whisker, it sports a trig column unseen until the last moment.

Slant down to the edge of the scar above Barrowfield Wood and make your way down to a large cairn which marks a distinctive walkers' cross-roads. Head left away from the rim to climb over the barren expanse on a well-engineered route that leads down the moderating eastern flank. After crossing a wall stile, you will soon arrive at the old racecourse. The starting box stands derelict and abandoned where once the sport of kings held sway. Now only sheep idly pass their time grazing on the succulent herbage casting a deprecating frown at those who would invade their territory.

Maintain a direct line across the course to join with Brigsteer Road. Turn left to cross the by-pass and head down into the outer suburbs of Kendal.

Cross the village green to the top of Beast Banks where bulls were once baited before being slaughtered. It was a firmly held belief among the populace that this obscene practice ensured a fresh and succulent taste to the meat.

Pass through a wall gap on the right which leads up onto Castle Howe which boasts a noble obelisk bearing the proud inscription *Sacred to Liberty*. It was erected in 1788 to the memory of 'The Glorious Revolution' which occurred a century before when William of Orange came to the throne following the abdication of James II. This motte and bailey type castle is best observed from below when the original defensive ramparts are still visible.

From this lofty perch, drop down to a narrow ginnel that has changed but little over the centuries bearing right to link with Captain French Lane. Turn down hill to arrive at Stricklandgate which is Kendal's main thoroughfare. As you stroll north, examine the array of burgage yards at your leisure.

Just beyond the impressive town hall, watch for the entrance to Angel Court on the right. Now occupied by the Halifax Building Society, these premises used to be the Angel Inn which acquired its celestial nomenclature through a strange occurrence that took place here in 1745.

In that year, Bonny Prince Charlie marched through Kendal on his way south to reclaim the throne of England for his father. Unbeknown to the young pretender, some of his more exuberant highland followers raided the inn. Finding it deserted except for an infant, the irate pillagers were suddenly confronted by an angel who prevented them kidnapping the helpless child. The heavenly guardian drove the rogues off and remained with the child until the frightened parents emerged from hiding.

Walk down the narrow alley into an open court that bears no relation to its grim past and make your way down to cross the River Kent by way of Miller Bridge. Take a stroll south down Aynham Road towards Parr Street where you turn left. Cross the old canal bridge and up to a stile giving access to the open grassy banks below Kendal Castle.

Ascend the inclined plane of this urban drumlin to make a circuit of the ruined castle walls and its dry moat. A magnificent site mounted high above the town, one wonders why the earlier fort was not positioned here overlooking all approaches. The main gate faced north and was entered by a drawbridge buttressed by a pair of solid towers.

Although in a sad state of neglect, municipal efforts are clearly in hand to preserve what little remains. With the help of a diagram set on a stone plinth, it is still possible to visualise the original splendour. Certainly it appears to have been a cheery place bringing a welcome display of extrovert pageantry to the daily grind of the ordinary citizens.

Katherine Parr is said to have enjoyed her happiest times in Kendal Castle, her hand-written *Book of Devotions* being preserved in the town hall. Perhaps that is why no evidence of a resident ghost has so far been revealed. After all, such apparitions are more at home where evil and nefarious deeds have encouraged their labours. A great pity. All castles deserve at least one. Any offers?

Head off north down the elongated tail of the drumlin. Glancing left to the old mills clustered at the terminus of the Lancaster Canal, I was reminded that Kendal is still the snuff capital of the United Kingdom. Production of this eccentric powder has been centred in the town for over two centuries and looks set to continue.

Blending of a variety of tobacco leaves results in all manner of snuffs being currently enjoyed by around half a million users in Britain alone. Miners in particular are especially partial to a pinch for clearing coal dust from their heads.

At the bottom of the grass bank, turn left down Castle Road and left again into Castle Street. After 200 metres, fork right down Ann Street. Turn left at the main road down Wildman Street where Castle Dairy is undoubtedly the hoariest building in sight.

Its rough cast exterior is of 16th century origin although the structure itself is known to be much older. Thought to have been a leper hospital, it has no associations with agriculture and is the oldest inhabited residence in Kendal. Close observation will reveal the smallest window in the town, possibly even the country.

Rumour has it that a secret passage once connected The Dairy with the Castle although none has yet been located. Could this be the derivation of the name?

Elsewhere in Wildman Street on a site once occupied by the Copper Kettle Cafe, a bizarre haunting was reported in 1981. The resident poltergeist used to douse the lights and even pushed the cafe proprietor down the stairs. Landing in a dishevelled heap on the floor, she claimed to feel the imprint of a hand on her back for two hours after. Work out which of the premises are involved and let me know.

At the end of the street, before Stramongate Bridge, turn right down Beezon Road to Sandes Avenue. Bear left over Victoria Bridge and head back to the traffic lights at Stricklandgate.

No greater contrast in scenic delectation can be experienced and relished on any other walk in this volume. From the dour slums of old Fellside to the open fell side of *The Scars*, a deep sense of the mysterious oozes from the vibrant pores of a town environment that has it all. Take the time to absorb this scintillating atmosphere where past and present fuse to a nebulous homogeneity.

26. North-west from Wrynose

Mysteries:	The Three Shires Stone GR 277027. Red Tarn GR 268037
Distance:	Short Walk 3 miles. With Crinkle Crags 5½ miles
Total height climbed:	Short Walk 1000 feet/305 metres. With Crinkle Crags 1950 feet/595 metres
Nearest centre:	Chapel Stile
Start & finish:	Plenty of roadside parking is available at the summit of Wrynose Pass.
Maps:	Ordnance Survey English Lakes, 1:25000, south-west area sheet.

Being the third highest road pass in the Lake District at 1290 feet/391 feet above sea level, Wrynose guarantees the attainment of a mountain summit with the minimum of effort. Provided, of course, that your velocipede manages the gear-crunching haul up from Little Langdale.

It is noteworthy that in 1902, Baddeley's *Guide to the Lake District* advised that "...Wrynose Pass is just traversible by vehicles [horse drawn carriages], but a snare to cyclists". During World War II, the road serving the pass was severely chewed up by military transport such as tanks on training exercises.

Once the tortuous route from valley level up to the *twisted headland* has been safely negotiated, locate the Three Shires Stone immediately below the highest point. Marking the focus where the counties of Lancashire, Westmorland and Cumberland meet, it appears strange that only the former is carved into the block of limestone. So what you may well inquire is the significance of *W F – 1816* on the other side?

The answer lies sixteen miles to the south-east in the village of Cartmel where a certain William Field lived. Being a stout-hearted and responsible fellow, William became a jack-of-all-trades as Bridgmaster, High Constable, Stamp Distributor, Priory Clerk and Will Maker. Clearly a personage of consequence in this tiny community who was well respected by all. In 1816, he commissioned the making of a stone pillar dedicated to his home county of Lancashire in which Cartmel then lay.

Sited close to the Cavendish Arms Hotel in the village, it remained there until William's death in 1860. Forgotten by all, it was his relatives who determined to carry out his original wish to erect the pillar on top of what was then known as Wrayene (from the 12th century interpretation of *pass of the stallions)*. Taken by horse and cart to Little Langdale and thence up the final gradient by a team of horses, it was eventually secured in its present position. No mean feat for people unaccustomed to travelling much beyond the next village.

Thereafter referred to as the Three Shires Stone, it replaced a trio of *brandreth stones* which were the original boundary markers. Set in a triangle, the 'three foot brandreth'(three-legged stool in old Norse), was mentioned as far back as 1610 on Saxton's map of Westmorland. Deeds relating to Cockley Beck Farm also allude to the stones, but there ultimate fate remains a mystery.

It would have been most disconcerting, however, to a character like William Field to witness the redrawing of Cumbria's boundaries that took place on 31st March 1974. Following this sacrifice to the machinations of bureaucracy, the Three Shires Stone became just a quaint memorial to the past along with Westmorland and Lancashire north of The Sands.

A wild and blustery situation, Wrynose Pass was an important staging post on the Roman road between Glanaventa (Ravenglass) and Galava (Ambleside). This ancient routeway can still be traced on the north side of the surfaced road as it descends to Fell Foot in Little Langdale.

The Walk

Immediately beyond the Three Shires Stone, take the track heading north-west up a gently graded slope that could easily be managed by your granny. Our immediate objective is the hollow between Cold Pike and Pike o' Blisco. As the path levels out, the lonely expanse of Red Tarn comes into view.

Here it was that Lanty Slee, that irreverent producer of illicit potato whiskey, is known to have secreted a cache of his potent brew. More of this rascally individual is to be found in Walk 22.

Assistance was secured from miners who wrested a precarious living from the haematite rock found near the tarn. Lanty was able to retain their valued support by ensuring a regular supply of liquid refreshment.

No doubt the welcome poteen fired up an internal central heating system, maintaining a continuous supply of ore during the harsh winter months. So everybody was happy – except, of course, the Excisemen.

Having assiduously searched the area on numerous occasions, I can positively affirm that no trace of the still or its output remains. But there again, maybe I've been looking in the wrong place.

Red Tarn is not without its mysterious happenings as a recent story related by that singularly quaint Clitheroe scribe Jessica Lofthouse suggests. Friends had reached the tarn by following a set of footprints outlined in the snow all the way from Wrynose Bottom. Upon their arrival at the frozen lake, the prints completely disappeared, nor was there a hole in the ice to indicate that an accident had occurred. The illusive stranger had simply vanished.

Could this have been the enigmatic *spirit* of Lanty Slee come to visit his old *haunt* just one last time? While exercising your mind on this bizarre conundrum, continue to the far end of the tarn and turn left to cross the outflow of Browney Gill. The path climbs the stony north flank of Cold Fell where it has been re-laid along the most eroded section.

Although necessary to prevent undue despoliation of routes pounded into submission by countless boots, these narrow stairways tend to remove the adventure from hill walking. By channelling people along set routes, the use of map and compass becomes a redundant skill. Perhaps once they are bedded in and blend more harmoniously with the accompanying terrain, acceptance by this rather cynical guide book writer will be more forthcoming.

If you decide to stick with the shorter walk, watch for a prominent cairn on the left when the gradient eases. Fork left and follow a thin trail up the northern shoulder of Cold Fell onto the crusty summit. Not one in a thousand hikers is likely to deviate from the main track to visit an unknown outlier that appears on casual acquaintance to offer little. An error of judgement rectified on this walk, and well worth the effort.

Should the allure of hard rock beckon irresistibly like a distracting siren, then by all means continue ahead. Passing left of Great Knott, the gently rising trail suddenly changes character as the first Crinkle of the extended fell known as Crinkle Crags is neared. The grassy plateau gives way to jagged crags which mark the start of what is undeniably the consummate ridge walk in all Lakeland.

This initial taster along a rock strewn apex finally descends to a neat col beyond which an apparently insurmountable crag wall soars aloft to prevent onward progress. Straight ahead, the steep gully that would otherwise have led unerringly to the highest Crinkle is blocked by a pair of hostile chock stones. But have faith, all is not lost. Climb between the sheer cliffs where a well-positioned set of holds enables this remarkable obstruction to be quite easily negotiated.

Perhaps discretion, or a muttering spouse, will persuade you that a safer route is likely to enhance your continued oxygen intake. If so, slant right to locate a thin path which avoids the exposed rock wall. Thereafter, a simple scramble up the tiered ledges of rock will bring you to the highest of the five Crinkles that comprise this splendid roller coaster terrain. Not surprisingly, there is an all-round first-class view to be savoured from the top. The Roof of England dominates the western prospect at the terminus of the continuos rim surrounding Upper Eskdale.

With thinly veiled promises to complete the entire ridge one day, look out for a salient cairn located twenty metres south-west of the summit. This indicates a chink in the armour of the south cliff. Make your way down the sinuous path angling left to return to the col below the *Bad Step*.

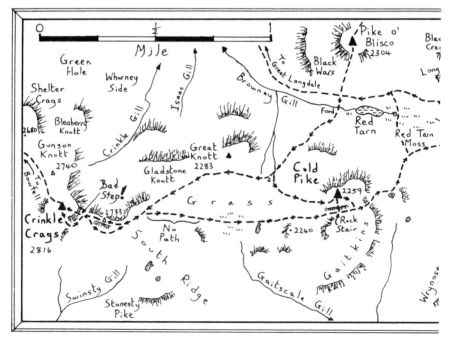

To maintain variety, avoid the rough climb back across the first Crinkle by forking right at the edge of the fractured rampart. Locate a thin trail that skirts below the crags to the west before merging into the outward track on the far side. Walk back down this for about 100 metres before forking right across the broad grassy saddle.

Initially pathless for the first quarter mile, aim in a general south-easterly direction until a thin trail is picked up in the grass. This crosses a marshy tract in mid course beyond which it passes close to a small tarn and then loops round making a rear approach to the clenched fist of Cold Fell. Nowhere are the gradients anything but gentle as the path homes in on the final scabrous pate.

Watch for a gap in the line of crags paralleling the path. This is marked by a cairn perched on a ledge. A narrow stairway provides access to the upper level which is followed by a simple stroll across undulating ground to the northerly of three summit cairns.

After enjoying the solitude of having a mountain peak to yourself, leave the summit barbican swinging west to rejoin the original path. Continue down the ridge towards a cluster of knotty outliers that mark the terminus of the spur above Wrynose Breast. On reaching the tarn, the path veers left down the grass slope forming the source of the infant River Duddon.

Swinging to the right down a grassy arete, the path soon dissolves into the tussocky arena of glacial moraine above Duddon Grains. You can quite easily join the outward track by maintaining an easterly bearing after crossing a feeder stream.

More of a challenge however, especially for those who have already conquered the *Bad Step*, is to carry on down the left side of the river gorge keeping well to the left of Rough Crags. There is no path until the lower slopes of the fellside are reached, close to a broken crag and abandoned sheep pen. Here, a path emerges in the grass that makes a beeline for the Pass.

Although the Three Shires Stone has become the scapegoat of political expediency, in essence it still marks the junction of this notable trio of ancient counties. Governments come and go, but the boundaries created by our forefathers will remain long after we have taken up the harp in St Peter's orchestra. Maybe the Friends of Real Lancashire will have some success in their endeavours to curb this wanton example of "cultural vandalism" by pressing for a reinstatement of the original boundary through public awareness on Lancashire Day.

Lastly and most important, I have been assured that not all of Lanty Slee's top grade moonshine was recovered from its niche somewhere close to Red Tarn. Maybe you will have more luck than I in locating, and sampling this unique tipple.

Red Tarn, where Lanty Slee hid one of his stills

27. Struggle up the Pass

Mysteries:	Kirkstone Pass, GR 402083; The Kirk Stone, GR 402086
Distance:	5½ miles
Total height climbed:	2000 feet/610 metres
Nearest centre:	Patterdale
Start & finish:	Descending the north side of Kirkstone Pass, watch for a distinct pull-in on both the left and right sides of the road at valley level. It is located at GR 402112 which lies 100 metres beyond the right-of-way where this walk begins.
Maps:	Ordnance Survey English Lakes 1:25000, south-east and north-east area sheets.

Hovering above Kirkstone Pass in threatening posture, Red Screes issues a salutary warning to all challengers aspiring to scale its craggy ramparts. Surging tiers of fractured rock peal off the soaring buttress. A frontal assault of this awesome redoubt is only possible from the plateau-like col opposite the Kirkstone Pass Inn.

Snaking up the rocky enclave, a thin trail eventually leads directly to the summit cairn over 1000 feet/303 metres above the Pass. This exhilarating route is made use of in reverse on this walk.

Highest of the road passes in Lakeland, Kirkstone presents few problems to motorists well served by turbo-injected superchargers. Modern vehicles float up the gradients with barely a hint of fatigue. But such was not always the case.

In the days when horsepower referred to the four-legged variety, the final hairpin ascent from Ambleside was well-named *The Struggle*. One petulant observer of the time poured scorn on the standard means of travel in poetic fashion thus:

> *He surely is an arrant ass*
> *Who pays to ride up Kirkstone Pass.*
> *He'll find in spite of all their talking,*
> *He'll have to walk, and pay for walking.*

There is no doubt that the landlord of the inn would have penned a more positive ode. Rampant thirsts so engendered on a hot summer's day were good for business.

They still are, especially on the day of the annual car pull from Ambleside. A lusty team of hardy *Schwartzeneggers* is required to haul a loaded vehicle up to the Pass at the end of a long hawser. Toughest job in the team has to be that of the helmsman who is forced to watch his colleagues revelling in the muscle-building exercise whilst working up a desperate taste for the amber nectar.

From the Patterdale side, the Pass is far more impressive. Savage turrets of ice-ravaged fell escalate on either flank. Walking back up the road to the signposted stile, the narrow cleft of the Pass at the valley apex presents a stirring tableau to behold. Cut off during the dark months of winter sometimes for weeks on end, I well remember one January back in 1978 after a particularly gruelling ascent of Dove Crag.

Negotiating a minibus up the final gradient was hairy indeed. Excessive wheel spin caused by the persistent snow fall was such that forward progress was being placed in jeopardy. Passengers in the back were vociferously encouraged with a high decibel output to bounce on the rear wheels. Only through the vigorous application of this tried and tested technique was the summit of the Pass safely reached. Our vehicle was the last over Kirkstone before the road was closed.

The Walk

Once in the field beyond the road wall, follow a set of arrowed marker-posts across the valley bottom until Kirkstone Beck is reached. Ahead, the threatening prow of Middle Dodd ploughs into the valley floor. This is certainly the most direct means of gaining the summit of Red Screes, but only for those secreting a booster rocket in their rucksacks.

Mere mortals aspiring to the more traditional form of portage should locate a handy boulder to cross the seething waters and aim for the ladder stile ahead. After crossing the wall, turn immediately right to cross Caiston Beck using a footbridge. Strike up the facing tree clad slope to join the packhorse route from Ambleside over Scandale Pass to Patterdale.

Pass through two gates in a small walled enclosure to begin the ascent of Caiston Glen. Initially alongside the in-take wall, the thin trail follows the right side of Caiston Beck up to the Pass, the final quarter mile being somewhat on the marshy side.

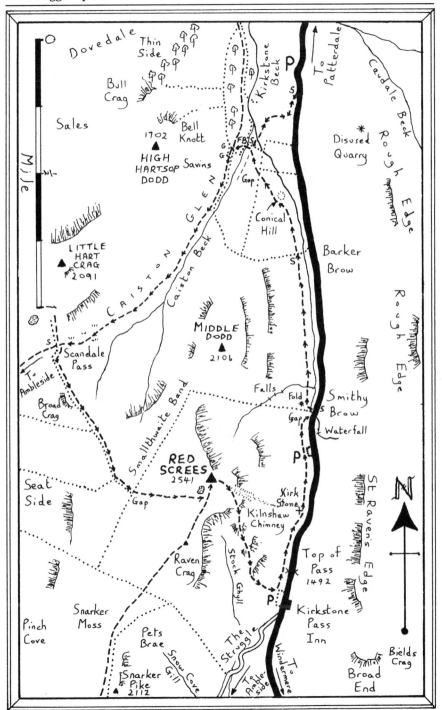

O

Dovedale

Thin Side

Bull Crag

Sales

Mile

½

Kirkstone Beck

P

To Patterdale

S

Caudale Beck

Rough Edge

Disused Quarry

1702 ▲ HIGH HARTSOP DODD

Bell Knott

FB

Savins

G
G

Gap

Conical Hill

Barker Brow

LITTLE HART CRAG 2091 ▲

CAISTON GLEN

Caiston Beck

S

Rough Edge

Scandale Pass

S

To Ambleside

Broad Crag

Smallthwaite Band

MIDDLE DODD 2106 ▲

Falls

Fold

Gap

Smithy Brow

Waterfall

P

Seat Side

Gap

RED SCREES 2541 ▲

Kilnshaw Chimney

Kirk Stone

St Raven's Edge

Raven Crag

Stock Ghyll

Top of Pass 1492

Pinch Cove

Snarker Moss

Pets Brae

Snow Cove Grill

The Struggle

P

Kirkstone Pass Inn

To Ambleside

To Windermere

Broad End

Bields Crag

Snarker Pike 2112 ▲

N

Enclosed in shadow, the dormant landscape of the Glen offered no clue to the bewitching pageant displayed to perfection across the whole arena of Scandale. Beyond the col on this particular winter's day, a dazzling brilliance reflected off the blanched terrain. Sunlight tickling the frosted shards of bracken gave the appearance of a diamond studded tiara – magical in its intensity. Truly a sight from which dreams are made.

A cross fell wall swoops down over Scandale Pass like a looping roller coaster. Here, it is necessary to head left up the western flank of Red Screes alongside the wall. Not especially steep, the steady unremitting plod is best accomplished in a characteristic *head down* manner. In this fashion, the low wall across Smaithwaite Band will be gained with the minimum of effort. Beyond the wall gap, slant half left over open ground to the crest of the elongated north-south whale-back ridge.

Our objective is the stone trig column clearly visible teetering on the rim overlooking Kirkstone Pass. On the day I arrived, the summit tarn was frozen harder than a champion conker. It revived memories of my first ascent many years previously. Snow thicker than a polar bear's overcoat inveigled the fells. Even so, numerous other visitors were already busy making slides across the opaque sheen. Today, there was nary another soul to disturb the blissful utopia of total solitude.

Peering down into the depths of the Pass, a thin wisp of smoke arrowed up from the inn. The faint hum of traffic breathing hard assailed the ears as I settled into the summit shelter for lunch. Only a pair of ravens, black as the devil's heart against the azure backcloth, circled purposefully in search of their food. Soon realising the fruitless nature of such a task, the frustrated hunters elicited a mournful caw before zooming off across the sterile landscape.

Care in copious quantities should be exercised on the steep descent to Kirkstone Pass. Now served by a thin trail, the route meanders down the craggy facade with the deep gouge of a massive armchair corrie on the right.

Originally, this climb to the summit made use of the stony gully known as Kilnshaw Chimney. A shifting spout of reddish scree pouring from the fissure has given the fell its more popular name of Red Screes. The current path now avoids this tiresome struggle.

Approaching the level concourse of the Pass, it is little wonder that the Troutbeck shepherds' meet was convened here in 1835. Whether its relocation from Racecourse Hill (High Street) stimulated the erection of the inn has never been admitted. Certainly the fell ponies would have been grateful for a diminution of their beer-toting responsibilities, without which the festivities would have rapidly ground to a halt.

At the base of the crag, make your way across to the car park. A faint path heading left should be followed to the top of the Pass. In 1805, Wordsworth passed this way with dense cloud enveloping the land. Although not displeased by the restricted view, he was distinctly aware that an otherwise mundane pile of stones *"might have been taken for a fragment of some monument of ancient grandeur ... transformed, dilated and distorted, as they are when seen through such a medium"*.

How then did he react when faced with the legendary Kirk Stone some quarter mile north from the top of the Pass? All is revealed in his ode to *The Pass of Kirkstone*, penned whilst returning to Grasmere Vale

The Kirk Stone, looking north to Brotherswater

following an autumn circuit of Ullswater. Therein, he referred to the pitch roof of the two metre chunk *"whose Church-like frame, Gives to the savage Pass its name"*.

Although 'kirk' originates from the Norse word *kirkja* meaning church, it is also used in reference to a heap of stones. When the inn was first excavated in 1846, an ancient burial mound was unearthed. Perhaps this is the origin of the Pass's nomenclature.

Alternative opinions suggest that the real name is *Kirrock Stone*, a flat slab upon which Druids performed their sacrificial rites. Whatever the basis, Kirkstone Pass can be a dangerous place.

Before the inn established a vital refuge for stranded travellers, a winter crossing of the Pass was always fraught with peril. One particularly harrowing tragedy occurred in 1839 when Ruth Ray with her baby infant ventured out from Patterdale during a virulent storm. Lashed by a ferocious blizzard, she sank down exhausted in the drifting snow.

Next morning, her distraught husband set out with his dog to search for Ruth. Skilled in the rescue of sheep, the canny hound soon discovered its mistress buried in a large drift on top of the Pass. Unfortunately, she had perished, but the child had survived warm and snug wrapped in Ruth's woollen shawl.

With these salutary thoughts in mind, continue down passed a fenced car park emerging onto the metalled road close to the fell wall. The protracted descent is well handled by modern braking systems. But many Victorian travellers on bicycles were not so lucky. Devoid of brakes as many contemporary velocipedes were, they frequently came to grief after spilling out of control on the tortuous run down to valley level.

Immediately beyond the wall, turn left down a flight of slate steps to join the permissive footpath. Hemmed in on either hand, the foaming torrent of Kirkstone Beck cuts a raucous bite though the choked bed of scree. Resume a steady amble down the rising flank of Middle Dodd soon crossing another wall stile opposite Barker Brow.

As the flat valley floor is neared, bear left around a conical mound ahead. The path crosses a broken wall and then arrives at the laddered stile negotiated on the outward journey. It is then a matter of merely retracing your steps across the in-take field following the way markers back to the main road.

More mysterious than the mythical Kirk Stone is the reasoning behind those who would choose to undertake this walk in reverse. Clearly only masochists and Clark Kent facsimiles would ignore the advice of their sagacious guide. To the rest, enjoy but take care.

28. Highway Robbery

Mystery:	Monkswell of Skelghyll, GR 394026
Distance:	6½ miles
Total height climbed:	1750 feet/534 metres
Nearest centre:	Ambleside
Start & finish:	Fork right off the main road as you enter Ambleside from the south up a narrow back lane located a quarter of a mile beyond the Waterhead traffic lights and opposite Hayes Garden Centre. Limited roadside parking is available on the left even on a busy Sunday. An official pay-as-you-stay car park is available 50 metres past the turn off.
Maps:	Ordnance Survey English Lakes 1:25000, south-east area sheet.

Towards the end of the 18th century, the burgeoning town of Ambleside boasted a pre-eminent situation at the head of England's longest lake. This served to encourage wealthy Victorians to settle in the town thus securing its future after the decline of the wool trade. Sheltered by the surrounding ring of mountains and commanding a southerly aspect, a new breed of traveller began to arrive. Tourists remain the principal source of revenue for the town, flocking into this honeypot from all points of the compass.

Today, the problems associated with such an influx especially that of traffic congestion on the region's busiest road have become acute with no apparent solutions in sight. Frequent tailbacks between Grasmere and Windermere ought to persuade you that Ambleside and its environs are best visited out of season.

Tourists primarily come to admire the scenic delectation on offer. Before this, Ambleside owed its prosperity to the rushing torrent of Stock Ghyll. Corn, bobbin, paper, bark and fulling mills lined its banks taking full advantage of this free source of power to establish the town as a major trading centre. The old streets and alleys behind the market place are still worth a visit retaining an authentic flavour which the rest of the town has abandoned.

In the Georgian period of the late 18th century, summer tourists coming to gaze upon this awesome mountain spectacle had other more sinister difficulties to contend with than traffic. Highwaymen who preyed upon horse-drawn carriages were a constant hazard for opulent travellers in these sparsely populated dales.

One such villain was a handsome rogue named Monkswell who robbed coaches and houses of the gentry assisted by a gang of heinous cut-throats. This mysterious scoundrel remained a thorn in the side of what law existed for many years until his arrogant lack of caution got the better of him. We will hear more of his illicit actions during the walk.

Overlooking the town like some artful predator lies Wansfell Pike, the knobbly termination of Stockdale's east ridge. Generally climbed directly from Ambleside by way of Stock Ghyll Force, this steep flank is best saved for the final descent towards the latter stages of the walk. Although somewhat Lilliputian in terms of overall height, the fell does indeed make a memorable objective for any walk.

It is perhaps noteworthy to mention at this point that the spelling of *ghyll* is peculiar to this small corner of Lakeland, the most celebrated of all – Dungeon Ghyll – lying but a short distance away down the Langdale Valley. More commonly, the Norse suffix of *gill* is added to denote a stream flowing down a ravine.

The Walk

To begin, take a stroll back down towards the main road forking left up the steep narrow access road to Skelghyll Wood. This right-of-way is metalled for the initial quarter mile after which it assumes the proportions of a real track. Ignore the access roads serving isolated mansions which slant left as the path enters the confines of Skelghyll Wood.

Becoming rougher as height is gained, the path bends to the left up the ravine of Stencher Beck. Cross the beck on a footbridge and continue through the wood alongside a wall. A gap on the right provides access to the rocky excrescence of Jenkin Crag which has offered an outstanding prospect across Lake Windermere for generations of visitors.

Return to the main path and head right leaving the sombre innards of Skelghyll Wood. Continue across the lower grass clad flanks of Wansfell towards the old farmstead of High Skelghyll. A pair of gates at either end of the rough farmyard will bring you onto the metalled

Low Skelghyll

access road. Follow this down over the tree-lined cutting of Hol Beck and so to the hideout employed by Monkswell at Low Skelghyll.

This wily cove led a secret life as a gentleman of substance visiting all the local mansions with the sole aim of casing them for future robberies. Being so close to existing settlements, it must appear odd to us that he and his sinister cabal of armed and masked confederates remained at large undetected for so long. Only by accident was the infamous career of Monkswell brought to an untimely conclusion.

Having been engaged in some degenerate intent, the gang returned to Low Skelghyll late one night. Unfortunately for them, one of the servants had become suspicious of the strange comings and goings at the house. He waited until all was quiet before investigating the stable, there to discover lathered horses covered in mud from a hard ride. But most damning of all, on the floor lay a highwayman's mask.

Monkswell realised his error the next day. Aware that the game was up, he disappeared with his entire gang. What became of the cunning brigand was witnessed at first hand exactly a year later by a local squire. Sir Michael Fleming of Rydal went to the trial of a certain Monkswell at the Old Bailey in London. Discovering it was his one-time house guest, Sir Michael related how the sly miscreant was convicted of

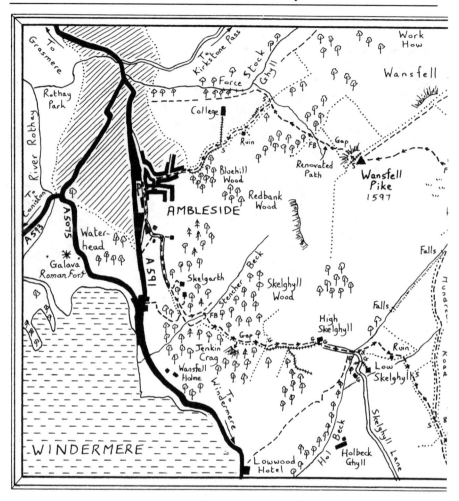

pursuing his old trade down south and was awarded a one-way trip to the hangman at Tyburn Tree.

The main house overlooking Windermere is well maintained but more intriguing is the stable on the right where the condemnatory evidence was found. It is unfortunate that the original rough track that made this house an isolated refuge for the Monkswell Gang has been replaced by a metalled affair.

Return to where the road crosses Hol Beck to pass through a stile and climb the banking on its right side. Accompany this clear path to

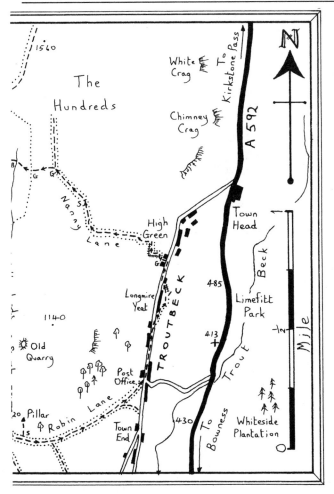

contour around the south shoulder of Wansfell. Beyond a stile, the Hundreds Road is joined and provides a much more realistic idea of how travel in the 18th century really was. This walled thoroughfare now becomes known as Robin Lane and descends gradually to the southern end of Troutbeck village.

Arriving at the post office, take a walk along the single main street which comprises an array of stone cottages and farms. These have grown up along a line of wells from which the communal water was once obtained, many of which were named after saints. By-passed by the main road from Windermere over Kirkstone Pass, the village became a prosperous community under the patronage of yeoman farmers during the 17th century.

Clerics also subsidised their meagre retainers by shepherding which brings to mind one story of a certain vicar of Troutbeck who met the Bishop of Carlisle whilst moving his sheep along the main street. When asked directions to the Parsonage, our worthy described the longer route to the Bishop who then continued on his way. Meanwhile, the vicar was able to get back to his abode and regale himself in the appropriate vestments to receive his guest. One can but surmise what the Bishop's reaction would have been had he recognised the parson.

Much of Troutbeck village remains unchanged with two notable buildings at either end. A quarter of a mile south of the post office is located a piece of Lakeland heritage preserved in the classic mould for all to appreciate. Town End is the best-known farmhouse in the District. It receives more visitors than the Mortal Man at the opposite extremity; this local hostelry was built in 1689 with the original designation of the White House Inn and sports a sign with the following rhyme:

> *O Mortal Man, that lives by bread,*
> *What is it makes thy nose so red?*
> *Thou silly fool, that looks't so pale,*
> *'Tis drinking Sally Birkett's ale.*

The wit who penned this caustic lyric clearly found the over-indulgence of his fellow drinkers a highly amusing source of entertainment. Painted by Julius Caesar Ibbotson of Clappersgate, the current offering is but a facsimile of the original.

Half way down the village street, take the track branching right behind a row of cottages known as Longmire Yeat. After returning to the main street close to a barn, look out for the start of Nanny lane on the left after a further hundred metres. Walled for much of its length, the initial steep zigzagging soon eases as the track climbs across the enclosed grazing of the Troutbeck Hundreds.

A quiet gently shelving stretch of fell, this eastern flank of Wansfell suffered one of the worst storms in living memory one hot June day in 1953. With the land sweltering under an oppressive blanket of heat, nature responded in characteristic Lakeland fashion by unleashing a torrential downpour.

But this was no ordinary rainstorm as the resulting devastation was to prove. Trees were snatched out by the roots and walls disintegrated. A howling gale swept the floodwaters down the ravaged fellside with calamitous effect, deluging the unprotected village and washing away the road. No amount of defensive action can withstand such potent strength when the forces of nature decide to get tough.

At the end of a straight section some 300 metres in length, take the gate on the left to follow a clear path through another gate and thence up the open fell onto the summit of Wansfell Pike. Not the highest point of the ridge, which lies a mile to the north-east, but certainly a supreme viewpoint for one of such diminutive stature.

Two miles northward lies Kirkstone Pass at the head of Stockdale with Red Screes soaring above the Inn. The most impressive vista, however, faces due west with the *Roof of England* dominating the skyline on a fine day. A minor fell in its own right, Wansfell Pike marks the southern extremity of an extensive ridge system feeding down from Caudale Moor.

The rocky bluff from which the Pike derives its name is unseen from this approach until the summit fence stile has been crossed. Only then does the abrupt downfall become apparent. This provides the main route from Ambleside and is well defined with a substantial portion having been re-laid to combat the severe erosion caused by booted pedestrians.

On a hot day, this steep little climb is not one to be attempted without copious reserves of water to hand. No such problems for us, however, on a swift descent which enters the lower scattering of open woodland after crossing a footbridge. On arriving at a wall barrier, head left down a grassy walled lane which brings you down past Blue Hill Wood into a recent housing development. Take the first left and then right to return to the start.

Modern Ambleside is very different from its humble origin as a *Norse shieling by the river sandbank.* Nor is it subjected to the rapacious attention of rascally highwaymen any longer. Although Monkswell would certainly recognise much of present day Ambleside, he would have long since been frightened off by the sheer volume of visitors who now come to wander its timeworn streets. Attacks in the future are much more likely to be of the climatic variety, if meteorological predictions for the next century are to be believed.

29. Quest for Dunmail

Mysteries:	Seat Sandal, GR 344115. Dunmail Raise, GR 327117
Distance:	5½ miles
Total height climbed:	2100 feet/640 metres
Nearest centre:	Grasmere
Start & finish:	Park on the open ground opposite the start of the Tongue Gill path close to Mill Bridge.
Maps:	Ordnance Survey English Lakes, 1:25000, north-east area sheet.

Sandwiched between Seat Sandal and Steel Fell astride the old county boundary, the Pass of Dunmail Raise is the fulcrum linking north and south Lakeland. At 238 metres, it is the lowest of the road passes and has been straightened to accommodate the rapid transit of modern traffic flows. It is still possible to make out the course of the original road veering away from the present route across Sutra Breast.

Without doubt, this is the busiest road in the Lake District requiring great care on the final section of this walk back to Mill Bridge. Certainly, it is difficult to imagine that in the early 19th century, William Wordsworth observed that the highway "*mounts, as you see, in mazes serpentine*".

The Walk

Once this main artery is abandoned at Mill Bridge in favour of the old pack horse trail, however, one quickly casts such latter-day distractions into abeyance to concentrate on the task in hand. After passing through the first gate, the rough track climbs steadily with the cutting of Tongue Gill dropping away steeply on the right. The wall on the left continues for half a mile until a second gate offers access to the open fell.

Ahead, the elongated shoulder blade known as Great Tongue splits the gill. Take the lesser known route following the left flank alongside Little Tongue Gill. The grass trail makes a direct ascent up to the rim of crags at the northern end of Great Tongue. Swing left initially then right to reach the upper edge with Seat Sandal filling the horizon directly ahead.

Accompany this clear track which cants in a left-hand arc into the upper valley. Here, the level concourse merges with a scree-choked path rising sharply from the valley of Tongue Gill. Much rejuvenated, this is now the most popular route of ascent. It then becomes necessary to pick your way through a boulder field under the glowering overhang of Gavel

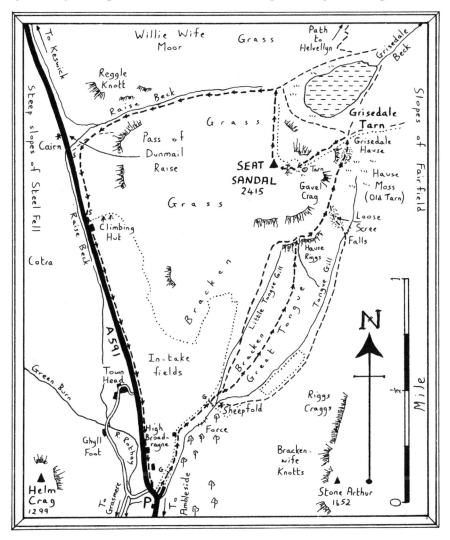

Crag. The route avoids the marshy depression of Hause Moss which forms the bed of an old tarn now silted up.

Cross the disintegrating wall at Grisedale Hause and turn immediately left to mount the steep east ridge of Seat Sandal. On the right, Grisedale Tarn nestles serenely in its corrie basin. Most travellers who pass this way will be unfamiliar with the mystical aura emanating from the inky waters. None could begin to imagine what strange secrets lie hidden beneath the placid calm. But more of this mystery later.

The thin path pursues a tortuous route up the craggy elbow parallel to the wall which is crossed as the gradient eases close to an insipid tarn. It is then but a simple stroll to the highest point. A broad grassy plateau sprinkled with stony outcrops, the summit of Seat Sandal lies close to the wall which crosses the top to descend the broad north facing mantle.

This old boundary line separating Cumberland and Westmorland makes an ideal shelter from the keen westerlies that howl their sad lament across the exposed tops. Akin to the baying of a thousand hounds from hell, the wind whistles and moans through the cracks and crannies. Is it little wonder that the mountain has long been regarded as a rendezvous for ghosts?

According to a certain Miss Attenborough of Ulverston whilst ascending the fell from Dollywaggon Pike, men's voices and a barking dog were clearly audible one fine afternoon. Expecting to meet a brace of shepherds once the summit was reached, she and her companion found themselves completely alone with no sign of anyone else nearby. A trick of the ether perhaps? Or does Sandulf, the Norse shepherd who gave his name to the mountain, still roam this lonely summer pasture in search of his lost flock?

Ponder upon this obscure conundrum whilst accompanying the wall down the easy grass-clad slopes to meet the source of Raise Beck. Turn left here to follow a rough track which descends the deeply notched fissure. Stick close to the left side of the rampant cataract as it whirls and thrashes among the chaos of rocks bound for the pass below.

After emerging from the scree-choked gully, the broad expanse of Dunmail Raise is revealed in all its bleak austerity. Few of the passing motorists will have the least notion that they are travelling over the site of the last great battle fought within the fastness of Cumbria.

Here occurred the final ignominious defeat of King Dunmail by the Saxon hoards in AD 945. After the battle, his body was interred by faithful henchmen beneath the pile of stones that marks the head of the pass. To prevent his mystical golden crown from falling into the hands of their enemies, the warriors ascended Raise Beck and cast it into Grisedale Tarn before fleeing eastward.

Legend purports that he who wears the enchanted crown has the right to again rule over the Kingdom of Cumbria. Each year, the followers of Dunmail retrieve the crown from the murky depths and thence descend to the stone monument there to bestir the entombed spirit beneath. Thus far, the muted cry has risen from the grave, "*Not yet, not yet, the time has not yet come. Wait awhile.*" Whereupon, the crown is returned to its mythical resting place until the time is right.

Will it be this year that Dunmail returns to claim his birthright? Who knows except the vanquished monarch himself.

Some authorities have suggested that the large cairn on top of the Raise is but one of many barrows (burial mounds) strewn about the Lake District and dating from the Bronze Age. Others claim that before an approaching conflict, each of the combatants placed a stone on the *Dun*, the victors retrieving one at the end.

Think hard on the legend of Dunmail whilst heading south towards

Dunmail Raise and the summit cairn

the climbing hut. With the constant passage of motor vehicles over the pass, it is somewhat difficult to conjure up perceptions of belligerent tribesmen battling to the death across this sombre reach. Such fables are, however, what provides the District with its captivating allure, and I for one approve of that.

A stile allows access to the main road just short of the stone climbing hut. Thereafter, a stroll down the straightened highway can be enlivened by the splendid prospect over the Vale of Grasmere ahead. The summit of Helm Crag in particular with its scabrous cap known as the *Howitzer* captures the eye. Half way down the incline to Mill Bridge, a parking area on the left gives some indication of the tortuous nature of the ascent to Dunmail Raise before the arrival of today's super-cars.

Here then is presented a walk with much to consider, especially if the legend surrounding the golden crown secreted in Grisedale Tarn possesses any semblance of truth. Ghosts there certainly are for those with the inclination to seek them out.

30. The Dark Sentinel of Whicham

Mysteries:	Whitbeck Church, GR 119840. Kirksanton, GR 140808
Distance:	8½ miles
Total height climbed:	1950 feet/595 metres
Nearest centre:	Silecroft
Start & finish:	Ample parking is available in the lay-by after turning north along the A595 close to Whitbeck.
Maps:	Ordnance Survey 1:25000 Pathfinder 625, Broughton-in-Furness.

It was once said that "*Nowt good ever came round Black Combe*". Whomsoever elicited this bold proposition might well have been referring to a particularly active winter whilst buried under an avalanche of the white stuff. Frozen wells, howling blizzards and Jack Frost in overdrive are apt to encourage such sentiments.

Being on the western fringe of Lakeland places Black Combe in the vanguard of prevailing winds scudding in off the Irish Sea. If low cloud is the order of the day, you can be sure that this errant gargantuan will receive his fair share in abundance. Indeed, the claim has been put forward by the good citizens of Millom that the mountain has its own inimitable weather system. Locals often enunciate that if you can see the Combe, it is going to rain and if you can't then it already is raining.

Remote from the main core, Black Combe is undoubtedly the senior citizen of Cumbria's south-west peninsula comprising the same geological characteristics as its more renowned cousin to the north. This outcropping of Skiddaw Slate presents a gently rounded appearance with a brittle flaky texture that is the oldest rock in the District.

Mountain status unfortunately is denied it by a mere 30 feet/9 metres although nobody can gainsay this noble aristocrat his true worth. Certainly nobody living in Millom is likely to deny that Black Combe possesses all those qualities in abundance that such an honour decrees.

Hovering above the town with evident relish, the sharpened prow like a Phoenician galley bears down as if to swallow the helpless settlement in its path. The south flank is dominated by ice-scoured recesses from which its name is derived. Fractured ramparts of crumbly slate contrast markedly with the sprawling wilderness behind.

Yet not all is gloomy that turns the sharp corner below Townend Knotts. Every season has its finer qualities and, for me, winter complete with its glittering white shroud is difficult to surpass. A time when stillness you can almost feel settles over the dormant landscape and nature takes a well-earned rest. Where silence incarnate pervades the atmosphere, unbroken save for the steady crunch of boots on the crisp layer of icing as you approach the summit of Black Combe.

The Walk

Make your way north along the lay-by taking the old track bearing right alongside the red sandstone church at Whitbeck. Tucked away beneath the dizzy heights above, it is rumoured to be the final resting place of only the deaf and the dumb.

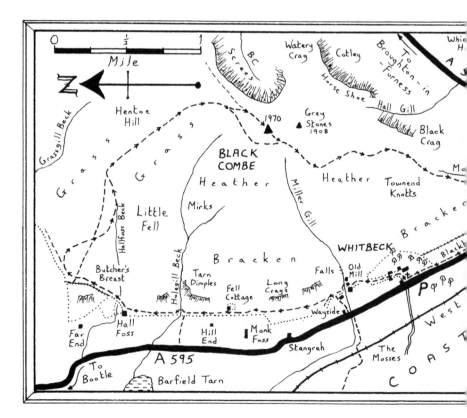

The church is also rumoured to be the final resting place for the Lady of Annaside who came from the hamlet of similar title some two miles up the coast. A stone effigy to this young maid of the noble Huddleston family stands bedecked in a wimple and veil alongside the ancient font. But little else now remains of the church's 13th century pedigree.

Remote from the major centres of population, it may come as no surprise that this coast was well versed in the wily craft of smuggling. Whitbeck Church was known to have harboured such contraband under the watchful eye of the incumbent of the day. On one occasion, the artful rogues had failed to dispose of their booty by the time Sunday arrived. To assist his cronies in their hour of need, the good reverend postponed the service for that day, doubtless selecting a keg of the finest French brandy for his trouble.

Paralleling the main road yet a million miles away in time, this ancient trail eventually allows access to the open fell at the point where Miller Gill cuts a hefty notch in the western flank of Black Combe.

Clattering down the ravine in a prattle of foaming spume, the silver cascade at one time powered the old mill alongside. Today, the spluttering turbulence passes by leaving the venerable wheel to muse about an age when such village communities hummed with activity.

After crossing Miller Gill where the track makes an acute kink, continue north veering away from the in-take wall on a gradual climb through the bracken. Beyond Fell Cottage, the path rejoins the wall to cross Holegill Beck after which the ruined farmhouse of Hall Foss is passed. At this point opposite Barfield Tarn, the route takes a sudden uphill surge.

The accompanying wall soon capitulates in favour of a fence which is followed until it merges with another wall coming up from valley level. Fork right off the main path to circle back heading south up the grassy sward of Little Fell. The way then bears left into a cutting as height is gained which marks the source of Hallfoss Beck. As the track fades in the bilberry and grass couches, maintain an eastward course to blend with another track climbing relentlessly across the bleak moorland expanse.

If you are unfortunate to be caught in mist, keep to

a south-easterly bearing to eventually arrive at the abrupt downfall of Blackcombe Screes. A mile of fractured rampart overshadows the lowering scooped hollows which give this mighty sprawl of fell its name in stark contrast to the planed aspect of the northern slopes.

Even when smoke is seen to rise up arrow straight from chimneys in the valley far below, a keen westerly always seems to gust across the exposed summit off the Irish Sea. Welcome relief comes in the form of a huge stone shelter near the trig column making an ideal spot for lunch.

Though still to savour the experience, I am reliably assured that the vista from such a high vantage point is the most far reaching in Lakeland. Certainly the western prospect over to the Isle of Man makes for an impressive tableau when Snaefell pokes a nonchalant thumb at the smudge of cloud hanging low over the island.

The mountain has been privy to a host of credits for the breadth of its panorama. Colonel Mudge, a 19th century surveyor with the Royal Artillery, claimed for it a more wide-ranging outlook than anywhere else in Britain. No less a personage than William Wordsworth himself depicted a graphic ode to the mountain in 1813 entitled: *View from the top of Black Combe*", two verses of which might wet the appetite for more

> *Close by the sea, lone sentinel,*
> *Black Combe his forward station keeps;*
> *He breaks the sea's tumultuous swell-*
> *And ponders o'er the level deeps.*
> *He listens to the bugle horn,*
> *Where Eskdale's lovely valley bends;*
> *Eyes Walney's early fields of corn;*
> *Sea-birds to Holker's woods he sends.*

Beyond the summit, cross a shallow depression housing a reedy tarn to reach the subsidiary summit of Grey Stones. This sports a man-made dais of substantial proportions in contrast to the main top. Unfortunately, it is beginning to disintegrate on one side due to the abseiling activities of some careless visitors. Head south-west to rejoin the main track bound for Whicham. The way is clearly defined and a delight to stroll down with blooming heather that brings a splash of purple to the dusky cant of the mountain.

Ahead, the close proximity of the sea gives the illusion of being able to dive straight in from on top of Townend Knotts. The steepest part of the descent follows the left flank of this knobbly promontory and so down alongside the dell of Moorgill Beck. Beyond a fence stile, continue ahead, passing right of Fell Brow to swing north-west through bracken below a parallel fence.

Below is the dispersed settlement of Whicham comprising a few scattered dwellings. It does, however, boast a church of great antiquity and a former grammar school of considerable repute. Indeed, Whicham is known to have been a prosperous community before the industrial revolution, having more yeoman farmers than any other parish in West Cumbria.

The story is told of a group of university men partaking of a meal at the John Bull Inn in the early 19th century. Thinking to make fun of the rustic landlord, they called for the bill in Latin. In the blink of a gnat's eye, it was presented in Greek and Hebrew as well as Latin. None of them could read the other two languages and they left soon after, well and truly confused.

Isolated from the main tourist centres, the small communities around the edges of Black Combe are firm believers in local tradition encouraging the handing on of diverting folk tales. One such fable involves the tiny enclave of Kirksanton which once possessed a proud church as the name *kirk* suggests. One day, the ground opened up and the church together with its environs disappeared into the bowels of the earth. Serving as the village green, an adjacent depression might well be the hallowed sight. Legend suggests that if you put your ear to the ground on a Sunday morning, the tolling of the lost church's bell can still be heard. Or does *kirk* merely refer to the *Giant's Grave Standing Stones* located half a mile to the north-west?

A thin trod leads down to the main road after which a mile of walking will return you to the lay-by. But what a mile! Only if you undertake this experience in mid September will the true nature of how Black Combe really acquired its name become apparent.

Never have I seen or tasted blackberries of the quality so ripe for picking as those found along this stretch of road. Gather and enjoy for here is nature's bountiful harvest awaiting the select few. Commandeer an array of suitable containers if your penchant is for an everlasting supply of blackberry & apple pies. Otherwise gorge at will.

Often overshadowed by more extrovert colleagues, the *Dark Sentinel of Whicham* stands proud and aloof in his remote domain. Nobody here dares to cock a snook at his lack of inches, nor scorns his plain attire. For Black Combe is the keystone, truly a Matterhorn over all he surveys.

More Lakeland walking guides from:

WALKING LAKELAND TRACKWAYS: the Eastern Lakes
Mike Cresswell
£6.95

WALKING THE HOWGILLS: Classic Rambles
Mary Welsh
£6.95

COUNTRY WALKS AROUND KENDAL
Mary Welsh
£6.95

NORTH LAKELAND WALKS WITH CHILDREN
Mary Welsh
£6.95

SOUTH LAKELAND WALKS WITH CHILDREN
Nick Lambert
£6.95

TEA SHOP WALKS IN THE LAKE DISTRICT
Jean Patefield
£6.95

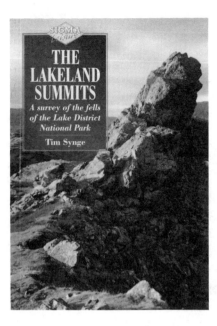

THE LAKELAND SUMMITS: a survey of the fells of the Lake District National Park
Tim Synge
£7.95

FULL DAYS ON THE LAKELAND FELLS: 25 challenging walks in the Lake District
Adrian Dixon
£7.95

STROLLING WITH STEAM: Walks along the Keswick Railway
Jan Darrall
£4.95

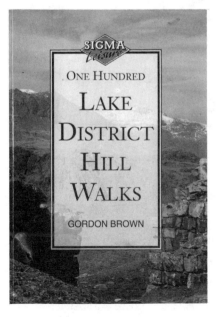

100 LAKE DISTRICT HILL WALKS
Gordon Brown
£7.95

LAKELAND WALKING: on the level
Norman Buckley
£6.95

MORE LAKELAND WALKING: on the level
Norman Buckley
£6.95

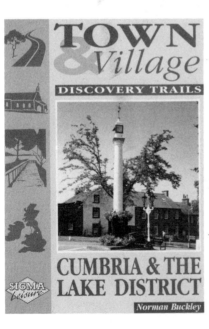